The

THREE FACES

Of

EVIL

UNMASKING THE FULL SPECTRUM OF
NARCISSISTIC ABUSE

CHRISTINE LOUIS DE CANONVILLE

black card
B O O K S

Author: Christine Louis de Canonville
Title: The Three Faces of Evil
ISBN: 978-1-77204-146-0
Category: PSYCHOLOGY/Psychotherapy/General

Publisher: Black Card Books
Division of Gerry Robert Enterprises Inc.
Suite 214, 5-18 Ringwood Drive
Stouffville, Ontario
Canada, L4A 0N2
International Calling: 1-647-361-8577
www.blackcardbooks.com

Printed in United Kingdom

The

THREE FACES

Of

EVIL

UNMASKING THE FULL SPECTRUM OF
NARCISSISTIC ABUSE

CHRISTINE LOUIS DE CANONVILLE

black card
BOOKS

TABLE OF CONTENTS

Foreword

Endorsements

Dedication

Acknowledgements

Chapter 01:   The Genesis Of "The Three Faces Of Evil" 1

Chapter 02:   From Darkness Into Light
A Glimpse Of My Personal Story 11

Chapter 03:   Revealing The "Good Wolf" 21

Chapter 04:   Revealing The "Bad Wolf" 31

Chapter 05:   The First Face Of Evil
The Profile Of A Narcissistic Personality Disorder 39

Chapter 06: The Second Face Of Evil
The Profile Of A Malignant Narcissistic Personality.. 53

Chapter 07: The Third Face Of Evil
The Profile Of A Psychopath 65

Chapter 08: Introduction To
Hare's Psychopathy Checklist (PCL-R) 77

Chapter 09: The Building Blocks Of The Psychopathic Character
The Emotional And Interpersonal Aspects 85

Chapter 10: The Building Blocks Of The Psychopathic Character
The Social Deviance Aspects 97

Suggested Reading 111

Resources: Websites 117

About The Author 119

Index 121

FOREWORD

"**A**coalface book on narcissistic personality disorder and the malign power of the narcissist has been absent for too long. In *The Three Faces Of Evil*, Christine Louis de Canonville brings a wealth of clinical and personal experience to bear on this much-misunderstood area. From narcissistic personality disorder, to malignant narcissism and psychopathy, this work will be an invaluable handbook for clinicians, students and interested observers alike."

—John O'Keeffe
Criminologist School of Psychology Trinity College, Dublin

ENDORSEMENTS

"Christine Louis de Canonville was recommended to me as the European expert on narcissism for my US-based radio show, *Mental Health News Radio*. Christine's guest appearance on the show has broken every record, with thousands of listeners within the first month of airing, and continues to attract new listeners every week. She is extremely down to earth, passionate and truly an expert on the topic of narcissism. Her work to educate those in the mental health profession about the proper treatment for survivors is ground-breaking. I truly believe her book and her work as a clinician will enforce the adoption of a necessary curriculum mandate for all professionals working with and for behavioural health."

—Kristin Walker
CEO of Behavioral Health Provider Solutions,
and Host of Mental Health News Radio

"At last! After years of standing as a beacon of hope in a world of fog and confusion for countless victims and survivors of narcissistic abuse through her website, *The Roadshow For Therapists*, Christine Louis de Canonville presents survivors and mental health professionals, whose responsibility is to help survivors, with a desperately needed roadmap for understanding the complex and poorly understood interrelationship between narcissistic personality disorder, malignant narcissism and psychopathy.

Throughout this book, Christine's lifetime of experience in the areas of psychology, medical anthropology, philosophy, sociology, metaphysics, spirituality, shamanic healing, theology, criminology, criminal psychology and forensic psychology, coupled with her courageous journey to healing as a survivor of psychopathic narcissistic abuse, come together to reveal an understanding like no other.

Christine's continued commitment to advocating on behalf of the "invisible victims" of psychopathic and narcissistic abuse around the world gives the rest of us who are advocating in our small corners of the world the information and drive to keep going. Thank you, Cihuatequiani!"

—**Michelle A. Mallon, MSW, LSW**
Faculty in the Computer Science Department
at Ohio State University, Columbus, Ohio

"My mother was a narcissistic exhibitionist. She hated me and abused me. Please read this book; it could save your life."

—Erin Pizzey
Activist and International Founder
of the First Refuge/Shelter Movement

"*The Three Faces Of Evil* takes the very complex topic of narcissistic abuse and makes it simple to understand and address. This book will be useful to both professionals and victims of abuse."

—Dr. Melissa Darmody
Clinical Director Towards Healing Counselling and Support Services
for Victims of Clerical Abuse Dublin, Ireland

Scan this QR code to
visit www.tinyurl.com/RadioInterview-1 and listen to the
author's radio interview by Kristin Sunanta Walker of
www.everythingehr.com about
Narcissistic Personality Disorder in Women.

DEDICATION

In memory of Gerard, who found life so hard, and
made it hard for others.

But through you, my dear brother,
I found my life's mission.

I hope, at last, that your spirit has found peace
in its spiritual home.

ACKNOWLEDGEMENTS

While this book is a personal statement based on my many years of experience as a psychotherapist and a victim of narcissistic abuse, I am indebted to all the clients and teachers I have had the privilege to work with while on my personal journey. I would especially like to thank my husband, Jacques Louis de Canonville, who kindly tells me that he came to this world to enable me to reach my fullest potential, and truly, he is the wind beneath my wings. Thank you to my gentle son, Sean-Pierre Louis de Canonville, who tirelessly helps me with literally everything technological, and who has the patience of a saint when I endlessly lose all my passwords for my computer.

Thank you to my wonderful sweet daughter, Sasha Louis de Canonville, a magnificent "animal whisperer" and behaviourist with the compassionate heart that always uplifts my spirit. Thank you to my son-in-law, Michael Rock, who provides me with beautiful pens and handmade chocolates to keep my thoughts flowing. I have been blessed with wonderful teachers and gifted friends who have inspired me along this path. Thank you to all my good friends, especially Michelle Mallon (social worker), who had the heartbreaking task of proofreading my manuscript. She did this mammoth job so quietly, and tenderly held my hand while encouraging me each step of the way. Dr. George Brownstone (psychiatrist), who graciously added his wide knowledge to this book. Kristin Sunanta Walker, host of *Mental Health News Radio,* who gave me my first ever radio interview, making it a huge success.

Shane Kelly, (Professional Services Manager of the IACP) who encouraged me to bring this knowledge to mental health professionals worldwide. To all my wonderful teachers, who saw the best in me, and graciously imparted their knowledge for making me a better person. Thank you Professor Ivor Browne (former Professor of Psychiatry at University College Dublin) for seeing the potential in me, and encouraging me to become a psychotherapist. Dr. Mary Creaner (Assistant Professor/Course Co-ordinator Trinity College Dublin), who saw my "steadfastness". Professor John O'Keeffe (Criminologist Trinity College Dublin), who took a chance and allowed me to lecture on his criminology course.

Emaho, a shaman, who challenged me to see life through "life's eyes", rather than through the eyes of the personality. Erin Pizzey, tireless activist and campaigner against narcissistic abuse, founder of the world's first refuge centre in the world and the Women's

Refuge Movement. Clive R. Boddy (Professor of Leadership and Organisation Behaviour), who fights the good fight against psychopathy in the workplace. Finally, I want to thank Black Card Books, especially Gerry Robert, Deborah Turton and Marybeth Haines, who nurtured me and my book every step of the way. They were midwives in attendance from its very conception, all the way to my giving birth to my firstborn book.

CHAPTER 1

THE GENESIS OF "THE THREE FACES OF EVIL"

An old Cherokee Indian told his grandson, "My son, there is a battle between two wolves inside us all. One is Evil: It is anger, jealousy, envy, greed, resentment, inferiority, lies, and ego. The other is Good: It is joy, peace, love, hope, humility, kindness, empathy, and truth." The boy thought about it, and asked, "Grandfather, which wolf wins?" The old man quietly replied, "The one you feed."
—Anonymous

We all have to grapple with these two wolves inside of us, and inevitably, one will win over the other to dominate our spirits. Most people choose to feed the Good Wolf who walks the path of growth and enlightenment. However, the

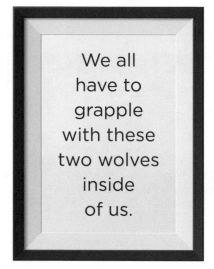

We all have to grapple with these two wolves inside of us.

narcissist chooses to feed the Bad Wolf, which has dire consequences for themselves and others. This especially applies to those on the high end of the narcissistic spectrum who are like rabid wolves dressed up in sheep's clothing, and who take immense sadistic pleasure from their predatory attacks on unsuspecting victims. I decided to write this book for several reasons. Firstly, because I have met the Bad Wolf several times in my own life. My first encounter with the Bad Wolf was in my early childhood where I grew up with a pathologically narcissistic sibling. Unbeknownst to me, this experience conditioned me in the narcissist's convoluted dance, priming me for being re-victimized throughout my life by other narcissists who were drawn to me like a moth to a flame.

Baffled by my childhood experience, I turned to various kinds of education for answers. I then went on my own personal journey of recovery, and finally I have become the wounded healer who helps navigate other survivors through the narcissistic maze for their recovery. Secondly, I have recently retired as a psychotherapist working one on one with victims of narcissistic abuse. My mission now is to work with other therapists, to pass on my experience, and to educate them so that they are better trained to work with the victims of this form of abuse, which, unfortunately, is on the increase.

In their book, *The Narcissism Epidemic,* Twenge and Campbell confirm that unhealthy narcissism has reached epidemic proportions and is spreading like wildfire across the globe. Visitors from 183 different countries have visited my website *(www.narcissisticbehavior.net),* and most of them are victims of narcissistic abuse looking for education on the subject. The last epidemic I witnessed

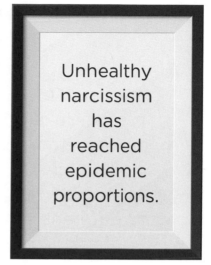

Unhealthy narcissism has reached epidemic proportions.

was the AIDS epidemic in the 1980s, which sprung us all into serious action for educating the masses. The education did not stop with adults; it was brought into schools and colleges, where sex classes were set up to teach teenagers and adults how to protect themselves from the deadly virus. It is time we took the same initiative with the whole topic of psychopathy (the study of the narcissist, malignant narcissist and the psychopath), and treat the subject in a similar manner.

We must educate everyone—the young and the old—to understand and recognise the disordered symptoms for staying safe when entering into relationships with others. It is only by understanding the subject and being able to identify (at least to some degree) the persistent antisocial behaviours in others that we can begin to protect ourselves from becoming victims. Although it is generally understood that men tend to score higher on the psychopathy scale, it is important to understand that women and children are catching up fast, and they too can cause untold damage in their relationships. As we shall see in the following

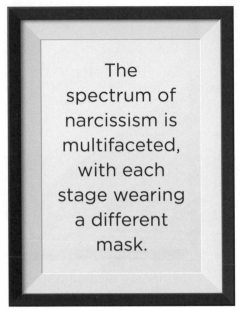

The spectrum of narcissism is multifaceted, with each stage wearing a different mask.

chapters, the spectrum of narcissism is multifaceted, with each stage wearing a different mask. Thirdly, when it comes to narcissistic abuse, I hope that this book will help survivors to figure out what kind of predator they were or are dealing with, and I shall do this by naming the different levels of narcissism, from the healthiest to the most pathological. The best way for protecting oneself against these predators is to know what you are dealing with and to be able to spot these predators before they spot you.

I can truly say that my own life has been my greatest teacher when it comes to understanding both the roles of the victim and the narcissistic perpetrator. It occurred to me that if it took me sixty years to figure all this out, then perhaps others were going through the same process. So, the task of this book, *The Three Faces Of Evil*, is to unmask the full spectrum of narcissism, from healthy narcissism to the three most pathological manifestations—narcissism, malignant narcissism and psychopathy. Technically these personalities are referred to in criminal psychology as the Dark Triad. Within these pages I will attempt to highlight the similarities, differences, and overlaps of all three personality types.

A useful way of understanding the psychology of the Dark Triad (NPD, MN and psychopathy) is through the Russian nesting dolls metaphor. The Russian doll system is a series of wooden figures that can be dismantled to reveal a series of several dolls (all similar, yet different in size) all fitting snugly encased into the largest doll. For the purpose of understanding the full spectrum of narcissism, imagine four dolls, with each doll representing a different level of narcissism, and its own particular, recognisable, overlapping pathology.

For example, the smallest doll represents healthy narcissism; the second slightly larger doll represents narcissistic personality disorder, and the third slightly larger doll represents the malignant narcissist. The largest doll combined with the other dolls represents the  psychopath, thus covering the whole spectrum of psychopathy within one Russian doll system—all encased into one complete "whole". The Russian doll system demonstrates nicely how each of these three unhealthy structures are in themselves complete, yet each fulcrum (level) of pathology distinguishes one from the other, depending on the trauma caused to each fulcrum, and how it twisted and distorted the individuals' growth as they went from childhood to adulthood. As the narcissistic individual moves from one level of narcissism into the next level of narcissism (i.e., from NPD to malignant narcissism), each level includes its predecessor, integrating it into the new and more pathological structure of self.

My journey started in my childhood, where I grew up in a family with a sibling who had what is often called a Jekyll and Hyde personality. Gerard had two distinct personalities: one was the loving Dr. Jekyll (the congenial Good Wolf persona), while the other was the wicked Mr. Hyde (the terrifying Bad Wolf persona); both of these distinctly different personalities made a relationship with my brother a very complicated dynamic. By the time Gerard was forty, the lovely Dr. Jekyll side of him was pretty much taken over by the tyrannical Mr. Hyde.

Looking back, Gerard's behaviour as a "fledgling psychopath" was apparent from a very young age. For example, he was a fire-bug, he thought it was very funny squirting petrol repeatedly on the coal fire and directing the flames towards my feet, where I sat petrified. He was also a chronic bed-wetter almost up into his teens. He displayed two out of three of the MacDonald Triad, the third one being animal cruelty; however I never witnessed him being cruel to animals. The triad states that any two of these three common behaviors during childhood can point to murder-prone children. Incidentally, many murderers start out causing "non-accidental injury" to animals in childhood (Zoosadism). Gerard was a loner in his teens, unengaged in school, acting out risky and impulsive behaviours, and often demonstrated a need for power and control. I was the youngest of five

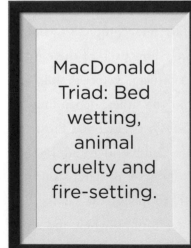

MacDonald Triad: Bed wetting, animal cruelty and fire-setting.

children, and Gerard was four years older than me. I adored him, and most of the time he was my best friend, a hero whom I loved and worshipped. However, there were times when it seemed that a switch went off in his head and he was overtaken by an impulse control disorder that made him an aggressive, sadistic monster that totally terrified me into submission.

Everyone remembers Gerard as a placid baby; apparently, he was the gentlest, most docile child out of all of us. However, he could be so stubborn when he did not want to do something, and once he'd made up his mind, nobody could shift it. My parents were both loving people, but I noticed that Gerard could be very possessive when it came to my mother. One time, when we were all adults, my sister brought my mother to Gerard's home for a visit. Everything was great until my sister suggested it was time to go. Gerard went into an instant unprovoked rage, beating my sister so badly about her head that she ended up in the hospital in the ICU.

I did not understand his jealousy around Mum, but I subsequently found out that my father was working away in England for the first two years of Gerard's life. As the baby, he had Mum all to himself. He even slept in her room during all this time; however, when Dad came home, Gerard was moved into another room with the other children, and his position with Mum was usurped by a stranger called "Dad". I think he experienced this as his core wound of abandonment and rejection by Mum, and never quite got over it. As a result, he constantly needed to be the centre of attention, yet terrified of further rejection, he opted for attention through negative controlling behaviour.

When Gerard went to school, he had a very bad time with the Christian Brothers (a religious community within the Catholic Church in Ireland), who have since been proved to be cruel and sadistic teachers. He hated school so much that he was always playing truant. These priests brutalised him; they truly were savages, but he refused to allow them to break his spirit. This only infuriated the priests even more. Although very bright and intelligent, he did very poorly at school, never reaching his true potential. This was a constant source of frustration and shame for him in his adult life, but he hid it behind a grandiose false self.

As time went by, Gerard's outbursts became more terrifying, and by the time he had reached his thirties, he had almost killed three of his siblings, putting each one in intensive care. I was one of those three. Of course, my whole family loved him and wanted to protect him. In reality, nobody knew what to do with the situation, and we were all too afraid to confront him because of his rages. So instead, we would lick our wounds for a while, forgive him, and basically go into denial that there really was a problem, praying to God that it would not happen again. I was baffled by Gerard's behaviour and wondered what could have gone so wrong to make this soft, loving individual act so terribly to his family. What was worse, he never seemed to feel any remorse or guilt for the damage and suffering he caused.

After Gerard settled down to have his own family, the pattern of pathological behaviour continued to be acted out, only now on his wife and children, making their lives a living nightmare of isolation, abuse, power and control to be endured daily. At some point, there was an incident when a gang of men attacked Gerard. I don't know how or why it happened, but they attacked him with chains and beat him around the head and body. They did a lot of damage, leaving him in a bad way, with a lot of injuries and a broken jaw. After that beating, his violence with his family became even more deranged. I believe there was further damage done to the frontal lobes of his brain, because after the gang incident, only the Bad Wolf persona remained.

It seems that the Good Wolf persona went into hiding after that episode. Finally, Gerard was far too dangerous for any of us to be around. With both my parents dead by this stage, we all, one by one (his three remaining siblings, wife and children) cut our ties and implemented "No Contact" for our own safety. Sadly, at age sixty, Gerard died alone in his apartment, his body not having been discovered for a week. Ironically, a family he had made friends with during the last ten years of his life (people I did not know, but met at his funeral) said that he was the most loving, gentle man, and they just could not understand why everyone was so afraid of him. I was relieved to know that the brother I had loved so much had found peace and happiness during those latter years, and that the lovely Dr. Jekyll persona had managed to survive and show his beautiful self once again. Apparently, some psychopaths do become calmer in older age.

CHAPTER 2

FROM DARKNESS INTO LIGHT
A Glimpse Of My Personal Story

"Nobody can be kinder than the narcissist while you
react to life in his own terms."
—Elizabeth Bowen

As I entered adulthood, I was perplexed as to what had happened to cause Gerard to behave in the way he did with me. In my early forties, I decided to pursue a degree in psychology. Of course, I know now that this was an unconscious need for answers. During that time (1991–1995), I was placed in the Post Traumatic Stress Disorder Unit within St. Brendan's Psychiatric Hospital in Dublin, Ireland. During those four years I was given the opportunity to become part of the team with Professor Ivor Browne. He was to become my greatest teacher in showing me how to work with victims of abuse and bring them from darkness into light. He taught me how victims of abuse could use unconscious mechanisms to block out the memories and ferocity of their trauma in order to go on living.

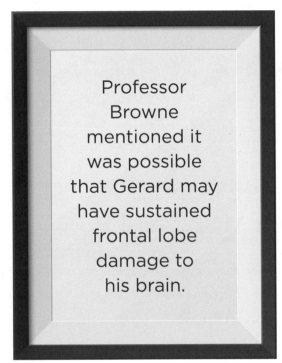

Professor
Browne
mentioned it
was possible
that Gerard may
have sustained
frontal lobe
damage to
his brain.

We were informally talking about Gerard one day when Professor Browne mentioned it was possible that Gerard may have sustained frontal lobe damage to his brain. At the time, I was not aware of what that could mean, and it was a further ten years before I was to discover the link between frontal lobe dysfunction, violent behaviour and the subject of psychopathy.

In a later discussion with my sister, I learned that Gerard had been in a terrible accident when he was only two years old. She was holding Gerard in her arms in front of an open upstairs window when he suddenly bounced on her knee.

Losing her grip, he toppled out of the window, falling down onto a concrete area below, hitting his forehead on the garden wall. Until that moment, I had never heard of this horrendous accident that in all probability had left Gerard with frontal lobe damage, as Professor Browne had suggested. Most people could see that Gerard and I got on really well together, but they did not know how his bullying, gaslighting mental abuse, and manipulative behaviours kept me in a state of high anxiety. One may wonder why I did not tell my parents; the truth is that I had learned not to tell tales on Gerard because there were always severe consequences even when I threatened to tell. In order to survive in the warzone that was my childhood home, I developed unconscious defense mechanisms.

True to form of most narcissists, Gerard would never take the blame for his behaviour, and invariably pass the blame onto me. For example, when he had one of his rages and hurt me, he would project the blame onto me, saying, "You should have known better than to have done that". Therefore, the conclusion was that it was my own fault I had gotten hurt. Consequently, I became overly responsible for keeping him happy— the dedicated "keeper of his moods", a "people pleaser" in the hopes of keeping myself safe. It worked quite well but at great expense to me, because in a way I was losing me. As he always insisted on being "the chap",

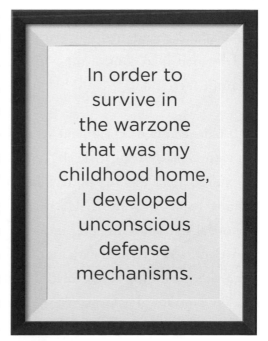

In order to survive in the warzone that was my childhood home, I developed unconscious defense mechanisms.

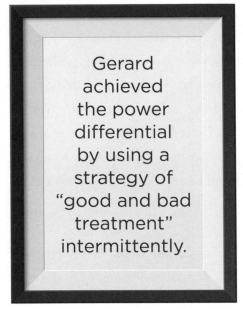

Gerard
achieved
the power
differential
by using a
strategy of
"good and bad
treatment"
intermittently.

the one who always got to win the game, while I became the passive player, "the Robin to his Batman" so to speak. I learned to stay in the shadows and never to shame or outshine him, because that could trigger his rage. When he was getting his own way, he was very loving towards me, and we could play happily for hours, it was sheer bliss. However, whenever I looked for my own way, the power imbalance would show itself. For example, if I were winning, he would refuse to continue the game, which left me feeling bewildered, rejected and abandoned. He learned the power of his rage young, and he used it to control me with fear, sending me into states of infantile regression.

This idealized attachment relationship between Gerard (with his emotional dysregulated self) and me (with my mis-attuned and frightened self) was the perfect mix for reinforcing the resulting trauma bond between us. He became the abusing guru, and me the obedient victim disciple, and in this way his first cult was born (which he later recreated with his own family). In Gerard's mind you were either with him or against him; his black and white thinking left no room for gray areas.

While Gerard grew in power and developed an inflated omnipotence, I, as his victim, became almost powerless and increasingly more dependent on him. To keep the power balance, Gerard had to keep absolute control over the dyadic relationship. He achieved the power differential by using a strategy of "good and bad treatment" intermittently. At times, he maltreated me to the point of terrorizing me, and at other times, he lavished me with acts of kindness, showering me with love, care and attention. Alternating between good and bad conditioning had the effect of subjecting me to alternating states of emotions where I would experience periods of aversive/negative arousal, and the relief/release associated with the aversive arousal (Dutton and Painter). Sometimes, when I felt overwhelmed and isolated, I would be triggered into a regressive mode where I returned to childish, infantile patterns of behaviour of bonding with my aggressor brother.

Such fear both immobilises and deepens the attachment bond forged in Stockholm syndrome. As one can imagine, these states of mind threw me into any number of uncomfortable inner conflicts where unconscious defense mechanisms were called for. There were times when I wondered if Gerard loved me or hated me. Because I did not like the discomfort of those conflicting thoughts, I would

> Such
> fear both
> immobilises
> and
> deepens the
> attachment
> bond forged
> in Stockholm
> syndrome.

rationalize his behaviour towards me was because he did love me, and wanted to make me stronger (of course, he always said he was being hard on me for my own good), and this rationalizing helped dissolve the cognitive dissonance I was experiencing. One day Gerard told me, "If you show your fear to people, then you put yourself in danger, and they will get you". I never did find out who "they" were; I suppose he was talking about the Christian Brothers in his school who did their best to break him. Gerard insisted that in order to be safe I had to overcome my fear, and he put me through the most stressful situations in order for me to master my fear responses. One day that stood out was when he placed a ladder precariously on the upstairs window ledge.

He then threw a ball up onto the roof and told me to go up the ladder and get it. I was about seven at the time, and even then I thought he was mad. I pointed out that the ladder was not secure and that I might fall and get killed. He was furious at me, calling me a fool, saying, "I am going to hold the ladder for you. Do you think I am stupid or something?" That was one of the days where I thought a beating was probably the best option of the two, so I started whining and refused to go out on the ledge. I will never forget what he said to me: "The greatest fear is fear itself".

How sad that a boy of eleven years of age was even thinking about such things! He did not beat me, but after this incident, he did step up a relentless campaign for getting me to a place where I no longer showed my fear. Some of the tactics he used were very brutal, like hitting me about the head and not allowing me to cry, otherwise he would humiliate me for being a "cry baby". Worse still, I was not allowed to put my hands up to defend myself; if I did, he went into a rage and things got much worse.

Eventually, I did manage to disconnect my fear responses from my facial expressions, separating what I was feeling on the inside from what I was showing on the outside. In fact, even to-day, when I am feeling frantic on the inside, I still manage to portray myself with a calm demeanor. Looking back, I think the worst thing was not the power and control Gerard exercised over me, but rather the oppression that denied my true self to flourish to its fullest throughout those years. But on the other hand, without that past, I would not have become a psychotherapist, or have had the passion for working with traumatised victims and understanding what they had experienced.

The problem with having been traumatised is that the repression associated with it can lead to what Freud called a "Repetition Compulsion". This is a pattern of behaviour where the victim unconsciously clings to people and situations that repeat some of the content experienced in their first abusive relationship. In total, I have been stung by four different narcissists. Finally, I realised that the common denominator in these four experiences was "me". So I asked myself, "What am I doing that is attracting this to me?" That question sent me on a journey of discovery that was quite surprising. Unfortunately, what is repressed cannot easily be remembered, and in some mysterious way we seem obliged to repeat the repressed "destiny neuroses" material (Freud) by acting it out as a contemporary experience through transference again and again.

It is almost as if what was terrifying in childhood, in some ways, becomes a source of attraction in adulthood, and gets acted out unconsciously, again and again, with the hope that this time it will all work out positively in the end. Freud called this unconscious desire to return to an earlier stage of experience as "repetition compulsion". Unfortunately, for victims of narcissistic abuse, this tends to cause re-victimization with other similar narcissistic personalities. For example, in my case, I found myself in abusive narcissistic relationships on four different occasions with different individuals. I also discovered that the interpersonal relationship with Gerard was indeed a very intense friendship (both frightening and exciting), and I was attracted to that intensity in other friendships later (but thankfully, never in romantic ones). It was as if when it came to friendships, my brain was hardwired towards narcissistic passionate risk-taking individuals who offered drama, excitement and intensity. In the beginning of these relationships (the idealizing phase), when full of seduction and attention, I felt alive, just as I did in the presence of Gerard's Good Wolf persona.

But when their Bad Wolf persona showed itself in the devaluing phase of the relationships, I went into all the same unconscious survival instincts I used with Gerard (i.e., becoming passive, confused, frightened, withdrawing, co-dependent, seeking approval in order to stay safe, etc.). Of course, as their source of narcissistic supply, my withdrawing would bring up the abandonment issues in these narcissists, sending them into a rage. In this way the whole cycle started over again, leaving me feeling very unsafe and bewildered, staying in the relationships far too long while trying to "fix" things, but only making things worse.

Through my own "repetition compulsion", I have finally discovered my repressed shadow self, dealt with it, and now I have no more need for the drama of another narcissist in my life. I am not angry with those three other painful narcissistic abuse experiences; they were a process I had to go through in order to resolve my earlier trauma. Actually, I am also grateful to them for helping me have the catharsis for getting healthier, thereby *completing* the *gestalt*.

Repetition Compulsion Trauma
- Some version of the past is always being repeated in the present.

- The amount of repetition is determined by the amount of the previous traumas that remains unresolved.

- "We are doomed to repeat what we do not remember." (Freud); in contemporary psychodynamic psychology, repetitive processes are called "enactments."

CHAPTER 3

REVEALING "THE GOOD WOLF"

"Had we not loved ourselves at all, we could never have been obliged to love anything. So that self-love is the basis of all love."
—T. Traherne, (1672)

Most people are inclined to think of all narcissistic behaviour as being pernicious, something that is always harmful to the self or other, but this is totally untrue. For that reason, it is important to distinguish between the healthiest form of narcissism and the most problematic forms of narcissism, not just in others, but also within our own selves. As we shall see, a person who sports a healthy narcissism is one who possesses a cohesive self-concept and positive self-regard, and is impervious to disintegration (Almaas, 1996). In contrast, individuals who have an unhealthy narcissism (the pathological and problematic form of narcissism) describes a person

21

> Most people
> are inclined
> to think of all
> narcissistic
> behaviour
> as being
> pernicious,
> something
> that is always
> harmful to the
> self or other,
> but this is
> totally untrue.

who is self-absorbed, has a highly inflated sense of self, has unrealistic ambitions and ideals, and is disconnected from others, which is magnified by their disconnection from their own self (Lowen, 1997).

Whereas individuals who have a low narcissism will be viewed as having little self-esteem; they appear painfully shy, lacking in confidence, insecure, hesitant, sensitive and fearful. Their energy is depressed, and they tend to have little presence in the world. In contrast, individuals who have a high narcissism (the pathological and problematic form of narcissism) describes a person who is self-absorbed, has a highly inflated sense of self, has unrealistic ambitions and ideals, and is disconnected from others, which is magnified by their disconnection from their own self (Lowen, 1977).

Narcissism is part and parcel of our humanness, an important vehicle for supporting our spiritual quest for the development of a true and authentic self as we journey through life. From our humble beginnings, it is our narcissistic tendencies that help navigate us through rites of passage as we develop from early childhood to mature adulthood, inviting us to move dynamically from self (ordinary self-consciousness of the human "ego") to Self (our higher consciousness) as we are steered towards enlightenment, and a consciousness of being.

> Narcissism is part and parcel of our humanness, an important vehicle for supporting our spiritual quest for the development of a true and authentic self.

One of the greatest challenges of man is to "know thyself", and the human heart has a constant longing to know its true nature, but the road to self-realisation is an arduous one. It requires patience and perseverance before the characteristics of the soul's steadfast joy, integrity and open-heartedness are revealed through the expression of authentic love (Agape).

When healthy narcissism is centered and grounded, an individual will experience appropriate levels of self-love; they can be real and loving with themselves, while at the same time show sensitivity for others. They will have the capacity to feel the full range of emotions that allows them to share in the emotional lives of others, and will be able to maintain long-standing, loving, mutually satisfying relationships. They can reach out in love to the beloved in a way that is unconditional and

One of the greatest challenges of man is to "know thyself".

mingles self-centredness with self-sacrifice, where there is equilibrium and equality. In such a romantic relationship, sexual contact goes beyond self-satisfaction to that of being an expression of gratitude of spirit, a gift of self to another. A healthy amount of narcissism allows a person to know their own strengths and limitations, and be able to laugh at their own imperfections without being swamped by feelings of self-loathing. They can gracefully accept compliments and praise without excessive ego inflation, and they have the capacity to accept themselves as they are, warts and all.

Their healthy sense of self-worth and self-esteem are constantly at their disposal, available for them to use whenever or however they wish; consequently, they feel safe and secure, and are able to have realistic expectations of themselves that fit comparatively with their abilities. Fully aware of being separate from others, they are freely able to enter into healthy, reciprocal relationships with balanced giving-and-taking with a generosity and humility of spirit.

Furthermore, healthy narcissism provides the means to separate truth from fantasy, reality from non-reality, and yet still allow the person to pursue their imagination and dreams in a way that leads to real accomplishments. Because they have faith in their own personal set of ideas and ideals, they are comfortable enough to play to the strengths of those around them without any sense of envy. Connection to one's healthy narcissism does away with the need to be envious of others' achievements; rather, it leads to admiring and embracing those people who reflect back one's own ideals, and prompts the desire to aspire to becoming even better.

In William Arthur Ward words, "When we seek to discover the best in others, we somehow bring out the best in ourselves". Actually, such a person can delight in the success of others and admire them as role models without having any need to make excessive demands on them. This creates within the individual the ability to bring into existence some quality that is uniquely theirs, something that allows them to leave their own personal stamp on the world. In this space, there is a healthy respect for both the giver and the receiver to retain their uniqueness and independence with each other, and to grow from the exchange.

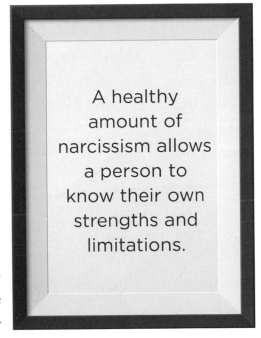

A healthy amount of narcissism allows a person to know their own strengths and limitations.

A person with healthy narcissism has grown up within a loving environment that provided them with a "good-enough" experience of a childhood that supported their self-esteem, provided healthy boundaries, adequate mirroring, empathy and challenges for building a high outward self-confidence in line with reality. Safe and secure in their own skin, they don't have to be always right, or suffer from crippling shame when they get things wrong. They have their own goals and values, which provide them with fulfillment and personal power, so they have no need to control, exploit or devalue others.

They are aware of their strengths and weaknesses, their gifts and talents, and they can reach out to others in a way that allows them to grow into their own particular gifts and talents without feeling any sense of threat from their external world. They treat others with empathy and respect, and this can be seen in how they show real concern for others, allowing them their opinions, thoughts and ideas.

Furthermore, they also have within themselves the confidence of knowing that they deserve to be treated with those same qualities in their relationships with others. They have no need to be jealous or envious of others, because they know that with the right effort they can achieve whatever it takes to be successful in life. They do not need to be the centre of attention, demanding the admiration of others at all times, or to live in the dream world of a grandiose false self, where they see themselves as superior and therefore entitled to special treatment. They are secure enough within their own selves to step back and allow others to shine. Everything they do is from a realistic sense of their personal abilities, rights and obligations due to their optimum access to their True Selves.

No matter what our age, we all have narcissistic needs in order to maintain our self-esteem. For example, it is normal for us to have a need to be understood, to be allowed to express our feelings, to be respected, valued, and recognised for who we are as unique individuals. However, when any person is going through a particularly stressful or painful time (e.g., such as the death of a loved one), they are likely to temporarily become more narcissistic or self-centered than usual; in effect, they regress temporarily to an infantile-narcissistic phase. This can be recognised in the way they become needier for attention, validation, mirroring, etc. But once the crisis has passed, the individual with normally healthy levels of narcissism will soon return to their baseline ability to reciprocate in their relationships once again.

When we speak of healthy narcissism, we are referring to someone who has invested energy into developing his or her genuine Self in order to lead an emotionally rich and productive satisfying adult life. Healthy, normal adult narcissism makes way for an individual's well-being, because it shows the synchronization between the Self (the true self) and the superego (the self-critical conscience), and the libidinal aggressive drives (the ability to receive gratification from others and the drive for impulse expression).

When the superego is fully developed and individualized, the individual's moral system is solid, and they are able to have stable, loving relationships with others. It is because of a healthy level of narcissism that the person can perfect themselves, which allows them to develop a realistic sense of their own intellect, sexual attraction, ability, intimacy, accomplishments, fulfillment, modesty, humbleness, etc.

Through mature, healthy narcissism, the person taps into the many levels of empathy within the self, levels that allow a person to experience a "love of love" that creates a sense of caring for themselves and others in the world. It is that sense of caring that allows the individual to demonstrate their social concerns and their interpersonal empathy for sharing in the genuine interests of others. With this presence of mind, the individual is also able to take personal responsibility when the things they do or say create problems for others. It is this aspect of oneself that whispers the invitation to embrace the elements of philanthropy and altruism within one's own heart for the good of all humanity. This type of person displays all the hallmarks of the evolutionary spectrum of being, and allows their consciousness to unfold in a way that reveals the human Spirit through positive behaviours that include self-possession, agreeableness, empathy, gratitude, affiliation, compassion and a need for intimacy—all signs of a healthy level of consciousness unfolding.

Scan this QR code to visit
www.tinyurl.com/CloudCuckooLand and
claim your FREE copy of
Living On Cloud Cuckoo Land.

CHAPTER 4

REVEALING "THE BAD WOLF"

"Deep within the narcissist's core being their soul cries out to be loved and accepted."
—Christine Louis de Canonville

There will be no surprise in hearing that unhealthy narcissism is the opposite of healthy narcissism. Unhealthy narcissism can be viewed on a continuum and comes in a very wide range, from very mild at the low end of the spectrum, to extremely severe at the high end of the spectrum. A person suffering from unhealthy narcissism—far from having a balanced love of a true self—compensates through a fictitious false self. The false self has little or no structural truthfulness of the self, so the unhealthy narcissist does not know how to distinguish their own self from that of the other, causing their addiction to a constant source of narcissistic supply (victims).

> Narcissism can be viewed on a continuum and comes in a very wide range.

Narcissistic supply provides all of the attention and excitement the narcissist craves (fame, celebrity, notoriety, infamy, admiration, flattery, acclaim, fear, repulsion, etc.). It does not matter whether the attention is positive or negative as long as the narcissist is centre stage. When deprived of narcissistic supply, a narcissist experiences symptoms similar to the withdrawal symptoms of a drug addict. They become delusional, agitated, helpless and emotionally unhinged, they disintegrate and crumble, and they may even experience a psychotic episode.

As we shall see later, Hare's (Professor of Criminal Psychology, and creator of the Psychopathy Checklist-Revised [PCL-R]), research has confirmed that there are anomalies in the brains of unhealthy, pathological narcissists that cause them to work differently from the rest of the population.

(The lack of synchronization between their self and their superego fails to develop a healthy conscience for proper living; without conscience, they feel little or no remorse or blame for anything they do. As their libidinal and aggressive drives are not balanced, they are unable to get gratification from others in the normal sense)(Morf and Rhodewalt, 2001). This leaves them highly impulsive and aggressive with an unstable sense of self-worth and self-esteem, leaving them in constant need for narcissistic supply. Because of their constant search to get their needs met, narcissists operate out of a range of addictive, negative behaviours that include competitiveness, being exploitative, Machiavellian deceitfulness, anger, hostility, a cynical mistrust of others, a lack of boundaries and rage (Morf, Rhodewalt, 2001; Sedikides, 2002). Their inflated egos make them overly confident, arrogant and needing a lot of attention from others. Their grandiosity often leads to them having unrealistic expectations of themselves that do not fit comparatively with their abilities.

> Narcissistic supply provides all of the attention and excitement the narcissist craves.

Unable to form their own ideas and ideals for themselves, they latch on to others out of envy, especially those who they respect as being superior, so that they can get that same sense of self from them. Unfortunately, those who are superior to the narcissist will unintentionally trigger the narcissist's feelings of lacking, causing them to feel shame.

Therefore, they get rid of any painful, shameful emotions by projecting them on to the other person, allowing themselves to feel superior. They are not looking for a mutually satisfying relationship with others where there is healthy giving-and-receiving. Narcissists take whatever they can from their relationships in order to feel better about themselves. Incapable of reaching a true reciprocal mutuality in any relationship, they either want someone to idealize for a while (one-down-manship), or someone to mirror back to them their "specialness" (one-upmanship). Either way, in time they will devalue the individual and discard them as an old shoe, but not until they have managed to get all the wear out of the victim that they want.)

> Narcissists are incapable of reaching true reciprocal mutuality in any relationship.

Ronningstam describes different types of unhealthy narcissism as characterized by three features: (1) dysregulated self-esteem, (2) dysregulated affect, and (3) interpersonal difficulties. All unhealthy narcissists have sensitive and fragile egos, and because they are behaviourally dysregulated (their emotional responses are so poorly modulated that they do not fall within the conventionally accepted range of emotive responses), they suffer from low self-esteem, which can be the cause of their conduct problems. Their behavioural dysregulation is associated with their reactive aggression.]

When it comes to any form of criticism (real or imagined), they are devastated by intense feelings of shame; they cannot cope with thoughts of being wrong, with failing or being defeated. They need to defend their fragile self-worth from such mortifying feelings and emotions at all times, so they develop a false persona of being special and unique. Their interpersonal relationships tend to be characterized by this need to preserve their self-esteem; this is often seen by their arrogant and haughty behaviour. If feelings of shame are triggered, the offender will be confronted with an intense violent rage that will become quite revengeful and sadistic, which will be acted upon without any sense of guilt or conscience. It is the unhealthy narcissist's inability to regulate affective responses to their internal or external stimuli (their feelings of shame, anger, envy, etc.) that dysregulates them, making them feel under constant threat (fight-or-flight response).

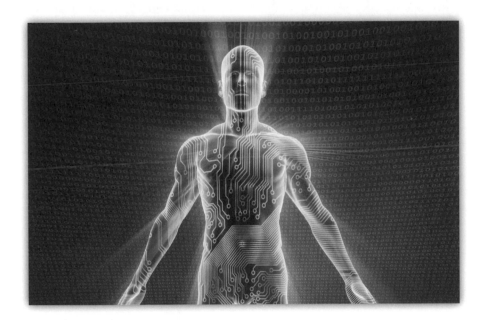

The activation of their automatic nervous system affects their behaviour, attention and arousal, making it almost impossible for them to regulate the negative effect. It is also the dysregulated affect that causes the instability that easily plunges the narcissist into self-loathing and extreme psychological pain, resulting in sudden outbursts of rage or punishing behaviour against the offender or situation.

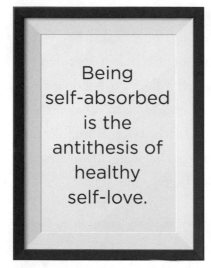

Being self-absorbed is the antithesis of healthy self-love.

The behaviourally dysregulated narcissist lacks remorse, but somehow they can always find an excuse that sufficiently convinces them that they did nothing wrong. As you can imagine, this creates interpersonal difficulties in all of their relationships. For example, in a normal romantic relationship there needs to be a sense of passion, commitment, intimacy, trust, respect and a willingness to be honest and transparent from both partners. Most intimate relationships share common goals and objectives that give life and longevity to the relationship. Unfortunately, narcissists are not known for respecting these qualities in their interpersonal relationships, thus leading to difficulties.

However, when a person's level of narcissism is unhealthy as a result of a disturbance in their sense of self, they become totally self-absorbed in their own self (to the exclusion of others). Being self-absorbed is the antithesis of healthy self-love; the person is self-centered, not other-centered, and thinks only about their own needs and wants, which they get through their incredible seduction, persuasion, projection and blaming; these are the hallmarks of the narcissist's manipulation. Narcissists are only happy when they are the centre of attention and getting perfect mirroring, perfect stroking, and perfect responses.

They always need to be in control, their worldview is always the only "right" one, and any attempt to get them to deviate will be taken as a personal affront to them, opening their core wound of rejection and abandonment. Whenever narcissists experience any threat of insult or injury (whether real or imagined), they typically withdraw or isolate themselves, provoking anxiety in others, then finally go into a rage that gives them back the control. Their need for revenge at having been slighted will call for extreme punishment of the offender.

In the following chapters, I will give a brief introduction to the three faces of evil, a flavour of The Dark Triad so to speak, which will put the reader on the trail for deeper research should they so wish.

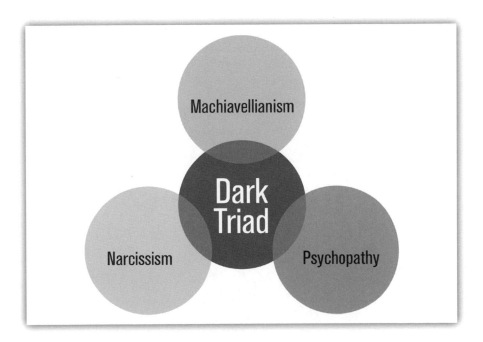

CHAPTER 5

THE FIRST FACE OF EVIL
The Profile Of A Narcissistic Personality Disorder

"The narcissist's display of self-love is in itself a sign that
he can't find a way adequately to love himself."
—Thomas Moore

The word "narcissism" roughly translates to mean, "inflated love of oneself", and it is termed a personality disorder. The key characteristic of narcissism is grandiosity, which leaves the narcissist with an inflated ego. Although these individuals can be tough-minded, superficial, exploitative and lacking empathy, their behaviours are usually an attempt to enhance their self-image for gaining attention, making them the First Face of Evil.

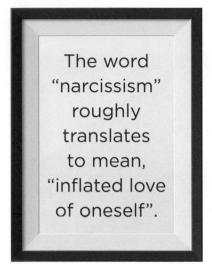

The word "narcissism" roughly translates to mean, "inflated love of oneself".

The American Diagnostic and Statistical Manual of Mental Disorders (DSM) specify nine diagnostic criteria for identifying narcissistic personality disorder (NPD). Before an individual can be diagnosed with having the disorder, they must fit five or more of the following nine descriptions.

Narcissistic Personality Disorder Criteria:

1. He or she has a grandiose sense of self-importance (exaggerates accomplishments and demands to be considered superior without real evidence of achievement).

2. He or she lives in a fantasy world of exceptional success, power, beauty, genius or "perfect" love.

3. They think of themselves as "special" or privileged, and that they can only be understood by other special or high-status people.

4. They demand excessive amounts of praise or admiration from others.

5. They feel entitled to automatic deference, compliance or favourable treatment from others.

6. They are exploitative towards others and take advantage of them.

7. They lack empathy and do not recognise or identify with others' feelings.

8. They are frequently envious of others and think others are envious of them.

9. They "have an attitude" or frequently act in haughty or arrogant ways.

Narcissistic personality disorder (NPD) is the most benign form of narcissism that refers to a set of character traits that involve self-admiration, self-centeredness and self-regard. Generally, people with this condition were born into dysfunctional families where they were either under-indulged or over-indulged as they moved through the psychosexual stages of development, which can leave the person's development arrested or fixated. Because the under-indulged child experiences the core wounds of abandonment and rejection, they withdraw into a grandiose fantasy

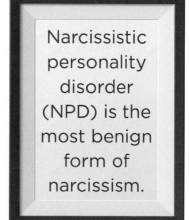

Narcissistic personality disorder (NPD) is the most benign form of narcissism.

> The American Diagnostic and Statistical Manual of Mental Disorders (DSM) specify nine diagnostic criteria for identifying narcissistic personality disorder (NPD).

world where they can feel loved and self-sufficient. When over-indulged, they become the princes and princesses that need constant attention. Unfortunately, these individuals haven't learned how to take the focus of evaluation from within themselves, so it comes from their external world through the narcissistic supply of others. However, although incredibly self-centered and self-aggrandizing, the narcissist with NPD has no malignancy. Generally, they do not have a history of childhood conduct disorder, nor criminality, and they have not learned to be ruthless at this level; therefore, they are not heinous predators. Narcissists present themselves as highly confident and superior individuals, but underneath the façade is an extremely fragile ego.

It is as if narcissists have a broken filter for viewing the world, so when they encounter problems, they view them through the lens of a wounded child, without the ability to think through all the possible consequences of acting through their destructive behaviours. To protect themselves, they develop an elaborate set of defense mechanisms to defend themselves from the outside world. Narcissists at this level suffer from "delusions of grandeur". (Their inflated sense of self-esteem leads them to believe that they are more important than they really are; consequently, they develop fantasies of power, wealth and omnipotence.) They view themselves as superior beings. (Their arrogant, haughty sense of entitlement leads them to think that they are above the normal rules of society, and therefore deserving of special treatment.) They brag and exaggerate about their own achievements, and will lie or fake their achievements whenever they feel there is a need. They demand constant praise and approval from others, and anyone failing to recognise their brilliance will be rejected, or even punished. To narcissists, others are inferior beings, therefore fair game for exploitation. With a limited, primitive empathy, they are free to exploit, devalue and prey on others with little or no remorse. They also lack good boundaries, and without healthy boundaries, they disregard normal limits of social interaction.

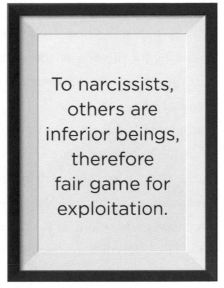

To narcissists, others are inferior beings, therefore fair game for exploitation.

Due to their high levels of insecurity, narcissists are very jealous and envious. Their jealousy is created by their fear of losing something, and their envy is the result of someone having something that they want or lack. Their jealousy works in two ways. First, it is the perfect smokescreen for discrediting anyone who confronts their behaviour head-on; to save face, the narcissist will announce to everyone that the person is simply jealous of them. Secondly, their jealousy leads them to believe that they have exclusive ownership over another, which is shattering for those in relationships with them. They don't trust any relationship, so they will accuse, interrogate, spy on, isolate, threaten, blame, and worse, use gaslighting techniques in every relationship. (Gaslighting is a form of psychological abuse narcissists use in order to instill an extreme sense of anxiety and confusion in their victims to the point where their victims no longer trust their own memory, perception or judgment.) Narcissists are also plagued with feelings of envy that are born out of their deep, emotional insecurities and poor sense of self-worth. Envy involves two people: the envier and the rival.

When the narcissist (the envier) sees someone (the rival) possessing something that they do not have, it provokes feelings of inadequacy and triggers their shame and resentful longing. When they experience this "lack" in themselves, it causes them to feel mortified, shamed and inferior. These distorted feelings cause them to experience narcissistic injury. Narcissistic injury refers to any threat (whether real or imagined) that the narcissist perceives is being done to their grandiose false self in any given moment. (With every narcissistic injury experienced by the narcissist's fragile ego, they will exhibit a reflexive urge towards a violent rage.)

Narcissists insist on associating with people they perceive as gifted. These flagrant rule-breakers use manipulation in order to ingratiate themselves to that person, and for a while, they will admire the person as being superior. They will want to rub shoulders with that person and get access into their social circle. By getting close to the person, they get a chance to study them, learn from them, mirror them, and then model their qualities as if they were their own. However, once they covet whatever it is that they wanted, they will then view that person as inferior. No longer of any use to them, they reject and discard the person off their radar screen. Before discarding their victim, they usually will have made sure to have become part of that person's circle of friends and consider it their right to use those friends in a similar way.

In order to protect themselves from feeling shame, narcissists use an unconscious primitive defense mechanism called "splitting". Splitting is a psychological mechanism that splits the narcissist's reality into two. Narcissists view the world in black-and-white thinking, where people (including their own self) are either all good or all bad, with no gray areas in between. In this way, the narcissist can split off from their disappointing, flawed true self in favour of their false self that they consider to be more acceptable to both themselves and the world.

Furthermore, any unacceptable flaws they experience in themselves are swiftly projected onto their victim or others. So when the narcissist sees a person as good, they can idealize them, and when they see a person as bad, they can devalue them.

It is as if they do not have the psychological maturity to accept the complexity that people can be a mix of both good and bad. So, for example, when their narcissistic supply is providing them with the attention they require, the person is accepted as ideal (all good), but when they fail in the task, the person is devalued (all bad). This is what happens when the narcissist splits their reality; suddenly, the victim falls from grace where they were idealized (i.e. where they were seen as loving, comforting, etc.) to being seen as their enemy (i.e. threatening, rejecting, engulfing, etc.), therefore they must be punished and controlled. Unfortunately, the narcissists' raging becomes their favourite tool for maintaining dominance and power in any relationship and leaves everyone walking on eggshells, afraid of the next outburst. If a narcissist actually apologizes, they do not do so out of responsibility or remorse, but because they are afraid that they are going to lose their source of supply. Once again, the delightful Dr. Jekyll persona returns to promise the moon and stars, and that the frightening Mr. Hyde will never return again. In that moment, the victim can see the vulnerability of the child, and they respond to it. Unfortunately, this is establishing a dangerous pattern that leads to an escalating cycle of violence and abuse.

Contrary to belief, narcissists at the level of NPD do feel emotions just like everyone else. They do experience guilt, love, passion, sadness, frustration, etc., but they seem to have a wonderful ability to repress their emotions so that they do not play much of a role in their lives. However, what is really missing is their ability to understand what other people are feeling; they lack empathy rather than conscience, which is most evident in their family home. The narcissists' stunted capacity to love, coupled with their sense of entitlement, leads to interpersonal difficulties. Their families are mere appendages for stroking the narcissists' ego (good objects to serve their needs, wants and desires, and to remove obstacles out of their way), and failure to do so will result in the blunt force of the narcissist's anger and rage. Even their children become their narcissistic supply, their own personal baubles that gain them attention through the child's gifts and talents. This lack of empathy affects the narcissist's life, causing them to become isolated from others, which they find very painful and confusing, leaving them feeling abandoned. For every narcissist, rejection opens up their core wound of abandonment, the very thing that they fear most. In a conversation I had with Dr. George Brownstone, psychiatrist and psychoanalyst, and a former consultant in forensic psychiatry to the Austrian Ministry of Justice, he states:

NPD is one form of a borderline personality organization, and all these people have in common: identity diffusion (an unclear and unstable sense of themselves and others); defences based on splitting (rather than repression) and projective identification (with untoward consequences for their partners); and a fear (separation anxiety), conscious and unconscious, of abandonment depression. Their all-or-none, black-or-white thinking leads them to fear that if they are anything less than perfectly fantastic and immeasurably attractive, they are worthless and unlovable, and will be abandoned and left to die (death by being starved of love). Consequently, they clamor for attention and affirmation that they're perfect—again, and necessarily, more perfect than anyone else. Their leitmotif: "There's two ways to see this: my way or it's wrong! You either agree, which makes us friends, or you don't agree, which makes you at least unworthy and possibly a dangerous enemy." They're incapable of healthy, warm, robust relationships, especially including love. Because of splitting, their object relations consist instead of idealization or devaluation— both pathological. A partner (lover, business, therapist, whatever) may at first be desirable because they, too, are endowed with perfection (the

formula: "I'm demonstrably perfect because I have such an obviously perfect—beautiful, gifted—partner"). But, usually sooner than later, the idealized partner's fantasized perfection leads to envy ("If they're so perfect, maybe they're more perfect than I am, and I envy that quality"), which, in turn, leads to hatred. Who was formerly perfect and wonderful undergoes a flip-flop devaluation, becoming perfectly unworthy, even horrible, and must be palpably denigrated, and, in extreme cases, destroyed. Depending on the degree of sociopathy (lack of superego or conscience, usually present, at least a bit), this will vary along a continuum from simple rejection, to controlling, to abuse, and ending with extremely malignant narcissism with remorseless murder.

Everybody is gratified by kind attention and affirmation of their lovability and worth; that's a basic and normal human need. But most people, endowed with a more or less realistic assessment of themselves and others, can successfully roll with the punches life deals out, and are able to maintain a generally robust peace within themselves and with those around them. Not so the abusive narcissist, whose abuse of others is the only tool at his/her disposal to try to keep him/herself on an even keel. The fact that it doesn't offer a robust resolution of his/her problems is lost on him/her. As Freud has said, "Neurotics are the stupidest people in the world. They don't learn by their mistakes." In any case, thinking about people with an NPD always calls to my mind the Persian parable of the scorpion and the turtle.

To sum up the narcissist in a nutshell: First, they're playing an unending game of "king of the mountain", but they're playing for keeps. Second, like psychopaths, the real crunch comes for them as they age and slowly lose their attractiveness and charm. Fearing they can no longer inveigle and deceive, terrified by the prospect of abandonment, they often become deeply depressed, or, alternatively, chronically somatically ill, leading to the need for constant medical attention and care. They seem to thrive on long hospitalizations, with a warm bed, three square meals a day, the camaraderie of other patients, and surrounded by concerned doctors and pretty nurses tending to their needs. Yet another attractive alternative for the more criminal types is prison, where they can also play the system, and which offers similar creature comforts and social benefits. All this, as much as possible, is at the state's cost.

Whereas the Diagnostic and Statistical Manual of Mental Disorders (DSM) explains the common garden-type narcissist well, to my mind, it is far too limited for the purpose of understanding the full scope of malignant narcissism and psychopathy, both of which are particularly virulent forms of narcissism.

TREATMENT

A narcissist rarely volunteers for therapy; when they do, it is likely to rid themselves of the emptiness that is dragging them down. Their main goal is to return to their grandiose state of omnipotence rather than getting awareness and implementing change. NPD is difficult to treat; the treatment centers around psychotherapy (combination of interpersonal and cognitive strategies), and in some instances medication (where there are symptoms of depression). However, it is difficult to keep narcissists in the long-term therapy that is required to reshape their personality patterns. For that reason there is a tendency towards a short-term therapy that concentrates on ameliorating acute troubles (e.g., depression) and increasing their self-esteem, thus reducing antagonistic feelings of entitlement, rather than dealing with the underlying chronic problems (temperament, anxiety disorders, mood disorders, delusional disorder, substance abuse, PTSD, etc.). Narcissists share surface similarities with histrionic, antisocial, paranoid and sadistic personalities, as seen in higher levels discussed in the following chapters.

CHAPTER 6

THE SECOND FACE OF EVIL
The Profile Of A Malignant Narcissistic Personality

"Malignant narcissism is characterised by an unsubmitted will.
All adults who are mentally healthy submit themselves to something
higher than themselves, be it God, truth or love."
—M.Scott Peck

The malignant narcissist (MN) is a completely different personality to the common garden-variety narcissist discussed in the previous chapter. Although malignant narcissists display all of the features of someone diagnosed with narcissistic personality disorder (i.e. their need for attention, admiration, their grandiose sense of self-importance, their preoccupation with the same fantasies of power, success and brilliance, their sense of entitlement, interpersonal exploitation, intense envy, pathological lying, a lack of empathy, etc.), they also present three more dangerous symptoms driven by "free will":

1. Antisocial behaviour, which makes them deviants with unruly impulses who defy all social conventions, and they only meet social obligations when it is self-serving.

2. Ego-syntonic sadism, which makes them predators with a tendency to destroy and dehumanize others.

3. Paranoia—their paranoid orientation may be the cause of their self-inflation, their mistrust of everyone, and viewing people as either enemies (to be devalued) or idols (to be idealize and used).

"Malignant narcissism is like NPD on pathological steroids."
—Dr. Otto Kernberg

In Erich Fromm's book, *The Heart of Man* (1964), Fromm described this form of narcissism as a severe mental disorder, calling it "the quintessence of evil". Otto Kernberg originated the term "malignant narcissism" to describe a syndrome of narcissism that went beyond NPD, saying, "Malignant narcissism is like NPD on pathological steroids". So adding the term "malignant" is done in order to indicate a more serious form of narcissism, making malignant narcissists the Second Face of Evil.

Outwardly, the malignant narcissist gives the appearance of being charismatic, charming, confident, self-sufficient and successful; however, their need for recognition is really derived from their underlying sense of insecurity and weakness. In order to hide their feelings of inferiority, they create an elaborate illusion of superiority that serves to build up their image of high-esteem they present to the world.

But in reality, they inwardly sport a fragile ego that leaves them vulnerable to shame and sensitive to any form of criticism, self-doubt or alienation. Under their persona hides a false self, a cold, predatory Machiavellian personality that is deeply envious of anyone who possesses anything that they lack, such as material possessions, education, money, power, success, likeability, intelligence, empathy, humility, etc.

They want what others have. This envy creates an insatiable lust within them, and with malevolent intent, they stalk their prey with chameleon-like adaptions in order to get what they want. Because they lack virtue, morality, humility, etc., they need to surround themselves with people who have those virtues intact. They will manipulate such people so that they can be in close proximity to them and then steal their identity, so that others will see them as having those same desirable qualities within their own self. They mirror that person's virtues with gusto, as if they were their own, and carry off the illusion to perfection, believing the sham to be real themselves. At the same time, they will deposit any unacceptable, hateful aspects of themselves onto that person.

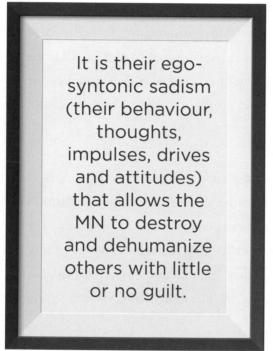

It is their ego-syntonic sadism (their behaviour, thoughts, impulses, drives and attitudes) that allows the MN to destroy and dehumanize others with little or no guilt.

With no conscience or guilt, they are convincingly believable to others. Once the malignant narcissist can get dominion over the person, they will lose all respect for the person, and the person will fall suddenly from their position as a superior being to that of an inferior being, to be controlled for however long the malignant narcissist needs to use them, and then the person is discarded. It is their ego-syntonic sadism (their behaviour, thoughts, impulses, drives and attitudes) that allows the MN to destroy and dehumanize others with little or no guilt.

And, with a disorganized superego, the MN lacks the amplitude for any empathy or genuine remorse as they do so. Regardless of the etiological factors that contribute to the development of malignant narcissism (whether it is biological, environmental, psychological and sociocultural factors), the symptoms are always the same: excessive self-sufficiency, excessive entitlement, being exploitive, exhibitionistic, authoritative, and feeling superior to the highest order.

Malignant narcissists are, without doubt, elaborately camouflaged predators who hunt for easy prey; they literally are the proverbial wolf in sheep's clothing that turns against others in a triumphant and destructive manner that is nothing less than pathological. They suffer from an inferiority complex, a compensatory egomania caused mainly by an underlying sense of insecurity and shame due to early childhood feelings of rejection, humiliation and debasing experiences.

Unlike the NPD individuals who were neglected as a child, the MN was also brutalized and humiliated. It seems that these experiences of aggression experienced as a child becomes integrated into a pathological self-structure where it gets expressed as a severe form of sadism and violence towards others.

They cannot abide to see another person be successful, get praise or receive attention—not even with their own children—and whenever it occurs, it is likely to trigger their "envy" button. Many MNs live vicariously through their children, putting the child in a "no-win" situation. For example, if the child is talented at a sport, the MN parent will control everything to do with the success of that sport; the child will be expected to perform above all expectations, with the parent taking the child's success or failure very personally. They will expect the child to achieve "gold medals"; a silver medal will be a source of disappointment to them, and likely to be treated as "first loser".

The internalized failure causes them narcissistic injury, triggering their rage, and the poor child is left wondering if they will ever be good enough. If the MN is unhappy in their marriage, because they see their children as extensions of their own self, they may feel justified in having incestuous relationship with their children. The child then becomes a narcissistic supply to take care of their emotional and sexual needs.

Malignant narcissism is not a disease, but rather it is an aspect of personality structure and functioning. So, the malignant narcissist differs from those suffering from NPD with their "excessive self-love"; they go beyond "love of self" to that of hurting other people physically, psychologically or financially. It is a more virulent form of narcissism, a syndrome that consists of a crossbreed of symptoms where behaviour becomes more and more disordered over time, leaving the MN needing higher levels of psychological gratification.

As they become more involved in reaching psychological gratification, they are apt to develop the antisocial, paranoid and schizoid aspects of their condition. However, as bad as all this is, Dr. Kernberg says that the malignant narcissist can still identify with other people, and even admire them at times. Unlike the psychopath, they still seem to have the capability to develop, admire and identify with powerful people as part of a cohesive "gang"; this permits them to have some level of loyalty and good object relationships towards others, even if they are their own comrades or disciples (i.e. being part of a gang or cult). However, they always view their victims as extensions of themselves, to be used to their own ends, and although full of contempt, cruelty and violence for their victims, the MN does not usually resort to killing in order to get their needs met. They have other ways of annihilating their victims, for example, through hatred, power and control.

Malignant narcissism falls somewhere between the NPD individual and the psychopath. When compared to the psychopath, the MN may have some semblance of conscience, but whether they always listen to their conscience is another question. However, they do know what they are doing, and they know they should not be doing it, but they do it anyway. They have such a need for total control that they will use any means necessary to get it and to keep it.

Unlike the basic narcissist, the MN does not really suffer from an inflated self-esteem. On the contrary, they despise themselves to the point that they disown their True Self, and instead they identify with a False self totally. They don't care how others view them; they don't need to be liked. Their aim is for others to fear or admire them, but most of all; they want people to obey them. They operate from a place of malevolent intent, with ill will towards others, true parasites who need to surround themselves with people to feed from.

Malignant narcissists think of themselves as highly independent, when the truth is that they are complete failures in a moral sense, and therefore highly co-dependent on virtuous people in order to project their own image of virtue. They prop themselves up on their victims by controlling them in order to feel powerful. The overt malignant narcissist particularly manages to steal virtue and substance from their profession, or by being members of certain clubs, organizations or charities. In these areas they are always looking to climb to the top of the ladder (i.e. the CEOs, head teachers, directors of training courses, counsellors, doctors, surgeons, cult leaders, etc.).

In these high-ranking positions, it is even easier to get closer to their prey with all the control in their hands. They see themselves as being the master of power and control, and they act that out to the highest degree. Control and power go hand in hand for the malignant narcissist, and in their everyday existences, they seek to dominate each individual and group with whom they interact. Their power is not "power with", but rather "power over", and it becomes their springboard to verbal and emotional abuse, especially in the home and workplace. The covert malignant narcissist often withdraws from the outside world.

Rather than looking for success from a career, they often retreat into the home where they dominate everyone within their circle of family and friends, creating a cult environment where they are the guru who orchestrates everything and everybody in the same way the overt narcissist does outside in the world.

Whether overt or covert, at first glance the MN appears to be very charismatic, educated, confident, charming and sociable. However, their interest in someone is not as innocent as it appears. Because of their need for attention, they see a person as a potential means of the narcissistic supply that they crave. In order to make themselves appear attractive, they invest a great deal of energy at putting their victim at ease, making them feel very safe, but this is their allurement at work.

They will make the person feel that they relate to everything that they say and do, and that they totally understand them, like an *anam cara* (a "soul-mate"). They will encourage the person to share their personal life with them, and they will appear to be really interested in what they have to say; of course, their victim will be seduced by all their worldly charms. But what the MN is really doing is enticing the person to become their source of supply, where they can control and manipulate in whatever way they see fit. When this is achieved, the MN feels really alive and powerful.

Their pathological confabulations are an important part of their weaponry. Their lies serve to salve their emotional wounds (or preventing wounds from being inflicted in the first place), prop-up their self-esteem, regulate their sense of self-worth, and buttress their

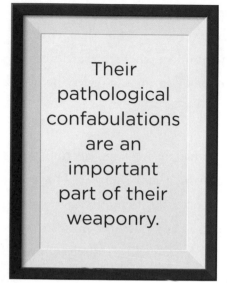

Their pathological confabulations are an important part of their weaponry.

self-image. According to Sam Vaknin (Author of *Malignant Self Love,* and a self-confessed narcissist) it is their lies that serve as organising principles in all the narcissists' social interactions.

The person who has been chosen as the means of narcissistic supply becomes a victim. Of course, the victim thinks they are having a meaningful relationship, but they are wrong. In reality, the person with whom they are dealing is an impostor, totally devoid of any empathy. They feel for nobody baring their own selves. The supply person serves only one purpose for the MN, and that is to lavish them with attention and benefits so that their ego is stroked and their needs are provided.

When they become bored with the game, the MN discards the narcissistic supply, leaving their victim confused, dazed and devastated. It will only be through "no contact" that the victim will begin to see how controlled every situation was—how everything was done through constant interrogation and unrealistic expectations, and how they were alienated from others in order to evoke obedience and respect for enhancing their narcissist's self-image even further. They will wince when they see how the MN used their power and control against them, and how they took immense pleasure in humiliating and demeaning them publicly.

TREATMENT

Generally, people with MN are high flyers who feel there is nothing wrong with them personally, so they would probably avoid therapy. According to Sam Vaknin, "These narcissists regard therapy as a competitive sport". This form of narcissist would see themselves as being far too superior and special to attend any therapist. If they did agree, chances are that it would be because they are attempting to manipulate the therapist for self-gain (i.e. to get a good report for the courts or workplace). However, there will always be a power struggle within the therapeutic relationship as they attempt to reduce the therapist to an inferior position. Therefore, as with all their other relationships, the MN will follow the usual protocol of idealizing, devaluing and discarding the therapist, thus protecting their grandiose omnipotent false self.

Even if the MN were willing, individual therapy would not be enough. What is required is a psychiatric therapeutic community that can provide the necessary intensive holding, corrective environment, and psychotropic medications used for the treatment of this personality disorder (Blair et al.). If therapy were to be anyway successful, then the MN would need to take full responsibility for their own insightful therapy by looking at their painful issues around their rage, envy, and hatred that remains locked up in the dungeon of their unconscious, and that seems very unlikely to happen. As bad as MN behaviour is, they are not capable of the cold-hearted actions of the psychopath that we shall look at next, the Third Face of Evil.

CHAPTER 7

THE THIRD FACE OF EVIL
The Profile Of A Psychopath

*"Narcissism is the over shadowing force in psychopathy,
the very root of all human evil."*
—Christine Louis de Canonville

Psychopathy, while not a formal diagnosis, is a complex personality disorder. It is the most severe, most extreme, and most virulent form of pathological narcissism imaginable, or as Hare calls it, "The mean side of the Dark Triad", a longitudinal condition that usually manifests in childhood. Psychopaths present with an extreme mix of narcissism, antisocial personality disorder, sadism, paranoia, and also severe brain abnormalities (i.e. caused by genetics, brain disease, or head injury).

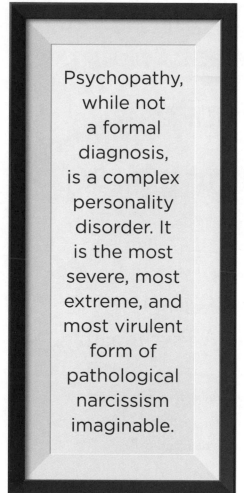

Psychopathy,
while not
a formal
diagnosis,
is a complex
personality
disorder. It
is the most
severe, most
extreme, and
most virulent
form of
pathological
narcissism
imaginable.

In short, psychopaths additionally suffer from anomalies of the brain that leave them emotionally and cognitively impaired, giving rise to attentional and behavioural abnormalities (i.e. impaired emotional learning, linguistic processing, socialization, moral reasoning and conscience) as seen in the development of psychopathy.

Psychopaths are therefore total predators, public enemy number one, whose brain damage leave them without the fear responses experienced by most people, making them the epitome of evil — the Third Face of Evil.

Psychopaths completely lack identification with other people and do not suffer any pangs of guilt for any of their actions, regardless of how repugnant others may find those actions. According to Dr. Kernberg, they cannot really experience normal emotions like love, joy and remorse. Emotion for them is like being colour blind. At best, they can only mimic human emotions, but they wear their masks of normalcy well.

Are psychopaths mad (criminally insane) or plain downright bad? The general opinion suggests that psychopaths are not mad; they are in touch with reality, and they don't experience delusions or become psychotic. They are aware of moral rules; therefore, they know that what they are doing is wrong. Technically, they are not mad, but rather clinically sane. This,

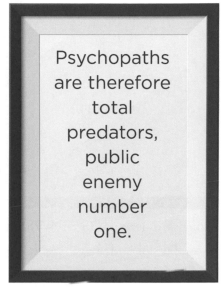

Psychopaths are therefore total predators, public enemy number one.

of course, is the great "Nature vs. Nurture" debate that has become the cornerstone of criminology that asks, "Are psychopaths born or made?" Nature concerns itself with the individual's innate qualities (i.e. genetics, chemical activity, hormone levels, physiology, IQ, etc.), while nurture is concerned with the individual's lived experience (i.e. perinatal matrices, environmental influences, bonding, socialization, socioeconomic status, deprivation, physical or emotional trauma, education, etc.).

Research shows that the determinants of psychopathy do reside within the individual; however, external influences determine the depth of the individual's psychopathy. Therefore, psychopathy emerges

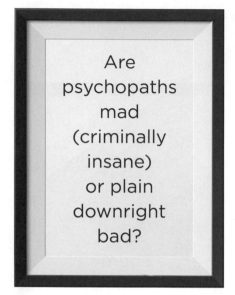

Are psychopaths mad (criminally insane) or plain downright bad?

from a complex interplay between biological factors in the brain and, social forces in the environment (Hare, 1999). The brains of psychopaths, for example, show low-level functioning of the prefrontal cortex. The prefrontal cortex is involved in regulating and controlling behaviour, damage to this area results in disinhibition, poor impulse control, lack of empathy, violent and aggressive behaviour, leaving them without an "emergency break". Anterior temporal lobe damage results in emotional unconcern, hostility, irresponsibility and disagreeableness. Damage to the amygdale results in boldness, low fear, and stress tolerance. Other factors that pre-dispose the individual to becoming a psychopath include reduced gray matter in the brain, low-activity Warrior Gene (MAO-A), and high risk variance of several genes.

Other social forces include early childhood environmental neglect and abuse (Fallon 2013). Essentially, psychopaths are understood to be missing a moral compass that leaves them totally devoid of a conscience. This can be recognised by their emotional callousness and antisocial behaviour. Lacking a conscience (plus an excessively active drive for reward) leaves the psychopath completely free of internal restraints, enabling them to act in a cold-blooded manner where they use everyone around them as pawns for achieving their needs.

Cinema has provided numerous accounts of the psychopath's personality in which they don't experience the normal range of emotions. Unfortunately, most movies look at the extreme cases of psychopathy, portraying the psychopath as being a pathological rapist or serial murderer. Furthermore, viewers are left with the picture that psychopaths are instantly recognisable by their frightening Dr. Jekyll and Mr. Hyde characteristics, such as seen by the Jack Nicholson character in the psychological horror movie, *The Shining*.

This ignorance is a misrepresentation of the true picture of the psychopath, and can leave the general population very misled and vulnerable to becoming a victim. Pure psychopaths really do exist, but they are very rare in society (1% of the population), and they usually end up incarcerated in either a mental or prison institution at some stage of their life because of their violent behaviour (e.g. Ian Brady and Myra Hindley, etc.). However, be warned, the majority of undiagnosed psychopaths fall into the more common form, called "the compensated psychopath", or "partial psychopath", and these are the people who live around us daily. Many of whom hold upstanding positions in society (Dr. Harold Shipman, Adolph Hitler), and may account for as high as 4% percent of the

> Psychopaths are understood to be missing a moral compass that leaves them totally devoid of a conscience.

population. As early as 1941, Dr. Hervey Cleckley, author of *The Mask of Sanity*, discussed the "partial psychopath" when he talked about "incomplete manifestations or suggestions of the disorder" in psychiatrists, physicians, businessmen, etc. More recently, Dr. Robert Hare referred to these compensated psychopaths as the "sub-clinical psychopath" (he was not talking about the 1% who are diagnosed killers and criminals, but the dangerous individuals that appear normal and live amongst us).

The subclinical type psychopath would score just below the top 25% maximum on Hare's Psychopathy Checklist (PCL–R) that is required for technically diagnosing a pure psychopath (that is, scoring between 30–40 on the scale). Whereas, a score of 26–30 places an individual at the high end of malignant narcissism, categorizing them, what Ronald Schouten calls an "almost psychopath".

Psychopathy confirms that the difference between the true psychopath and the compensated psychopath (the almost psychopath) is really just one of degree. The difference is seen in the latter's frequency and intensity of their inappropriate behaviour and emotional dysfunction towards others, plus their ability to keep up a better and more consistent outward appearance of being normal. Since they seem to maintain a place in society just below the radar of the law, you are far more likely to run into this subclinical psychopath than the pure psychopath.

A psychopath can be anybody—a family member, a neighbour, a friend, a co-worker, a high-authority figure or a homeless person. In reality, psychopathy touches almost all of us, male and female. So widespread is this problem that Dr. Robert Hare tells us that these callous personalities can be found not only in serial killers and rapists, but in thieves, swindlers, conmen, wife beaters, white-collar workers, stockbrokers, child abusers, gang members, disbarred lawyers, drug barons, professional gamblers, members of organized crime, doctors who lost their license, terrorists, cult leaders, mercenaries, unscrupulous business people, etc. It is estimated that in Britain 1 in 200 are psychopaths; in America, it is 1 in 100, and the vast majority are neither criminal or in prison.

On first meeting a psychopath, they will most likely make a distinct, positive impression on you. You are likely to find them charming, incredible communicators, energetic, friendly, interesting and exciting, but most of all they appear to be "normal". This mask of normalcy is all part of the manipulation the psychopath uses in order to "reel you in". They almost always create chaos for others by violating social norms, but the mystery is how so many people get taken in by them. There comes a time in the therapy room when each victim asks that question of themselves, "How could I not have seen what was happening? What's wrong with me? I must be stupid."

William March, in his book, *The Bad Seed* (1954), gives a good reason as to how so many people are dupable. He said: "Good people are rarely suspicious: they cannot imagine others doing the things they themselves are incapable of doing; usually they accept the un-dramatic solution as the correct one, and let matters rest there. Then too, the normal are inclined to visualize the psychopath as one who's as monstrous in appearance as he is in mind, which is about as far from the truth as one could get.

"These monsters of real life usually look and behave in a more normal manner than their actually normal brothers and sisters; they present a more convincing picture of virtue than virtue presents of itself—just as the wax rosebud or the plastic peach seemed more perfect to the eye, more what the mind thought a rosebud or a peach should be, than the imperfect original from which it had been modeled".

Nobody wants to believe that such evil exists in the world. At a time when human consciousness is raising, it is more comfortable for us to believe that people are inherently good rather than intrinsically bad. But therein lays the problem. People need to wake up, not be naïve, and come out of their comfort zone of denial. It is time to be realistic and admit that the "good wolf" and "bad wolf" is part of the human condition. We must take stock of our own narcissistic traits, and equally not be blind to those aspects in others.

When it comes to NPD, malignant narcissism and psychopathy, Kernberg says, "All three levels of narcissistic behaviour share the common threads of extreme self-absorption and insensitivity that often result in a trail of victims' emotional wreckage left in the narcissist's wake. If we are to protect ourselves from these narcissistic personality types, then we have to get away from our limiting beliefs that hold on to the sensational model of the "black" psychopath being the only type of narcissist that is dangerous. We need to educate ourselves on the subject of the various degrees of narcissistic behaviour; otherwise we are always going to be at the mercy of our ignorance, leaving ourselves vulnerable whenever confronted with pathological narcissism".

TREATMENT

Research shows that psychopaths are exponentially responsible for most crime, violence and murder in society, so in order to protect people we have to find an effective cure for psychopathy. Although the cause of psychopathy has not really been established, RMI scans show it may be due to physical factors of abnormal brain connectivity and chemistry, especially in the areas of the amygdala and orbital/ventrolateral frontal cortex, leaving the person cold, calculating and ruthless. However, the treatability of psychopaths has caused a considerable amount of controversy, with many experts saying that psychopaths can be trained but not cured. However, psychiatrist Dr. Bob Johnson sees these predators, not so much as faulty machines, but suffering from the effects of faulty programming due to the impact of early trauma, which he names "frozen terror". He believes a therapy that acts to unfreeze the trauma can be very successful for working through painful childhood memories, which allows the individual to grow up and bring about change in their personality and behaviour.

However, Dr. Robert Hare, an expert on psychopathy, seems to think that not only is therapy futile with these individuals, but it actually exacerbates the condition. Through the therapy process, these individuals learn how to fake empathy and other normal responses, giving them even more control over manipulating their victims. Empirical research may be the key to understanding the etiology of psychopathy, and if these anomalies are detected during early childhood and nurtured by a warm, loving environment, psychopathy may be avoidable before the brain becomes hard-wired for entrenched violence (Salekin, 2002; Wong and Hare 2005), thus preventing the development of the spectrum of psychopathy in adulthood (Morley and Hall, 2003; Fallon, 2013).

Neuroscientists are working on new treatments for protecting us against psychopaths. According to Professor Adrian Raine, within the next ten years, science will develop a way of replacing dysfunctional brain mechanisms with brain implants (microchips) that will change the wiring structures of the brains of psychopaths who cannot otherwise be treated. Without doubt, this research will raise new ethical and moral dilemmas, such as, "Is our penal system too hard on these individuals", or "Is it right that we change the wiring structures of people's brains?" Or will it be the overriding cost of trying to deal with the fallout of psychopathy that will be the deciding factor in the end?

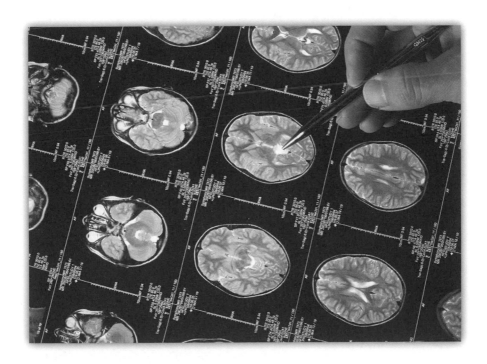

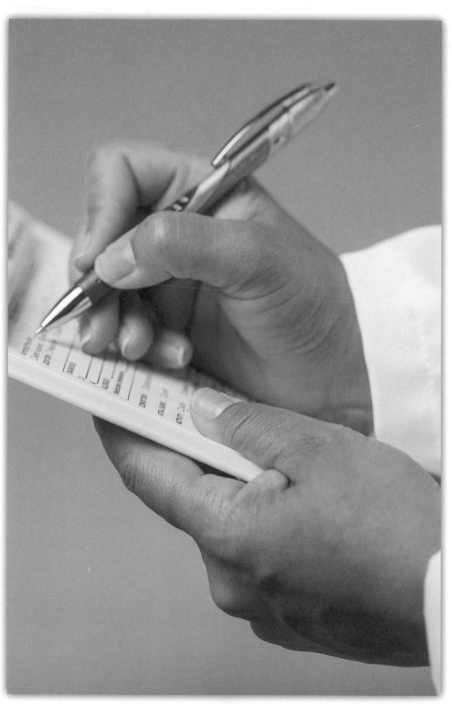

CHAPTER 8

INTRODUCTION TO HARE'S PSYCHOPATHY CHECKLIST (PCL-R)

"How can evil be integrated? There is only one possibility: to assimilate it, that is to say, raise it to the level of consciousness."
—C.G. Jung

Whereas the American Diagnostic and Statistical Manual of Mental Disorders (DSM) is useful in that it specifies nine diagnostic criteria for identifying NPD (as seen in chapter 5), it falls shy when it comes to understanding the full spectrum of narcissism. Until such time that the DSM includes malignant narcissism and psychopathy as precise and unique disorders, it is far too limited for gaining an understanding of the full spectrum of narcissistic abuse.

> Hare's Psychopathy Checklist-Revised (PCL-R). It is currently being used by many health professionals worldwide as "the gold standard" methodology for assessing an individual's psychopathic or antisocial tendencies.

Although the Russian doll metaphor (discussed in chapter 1) is useful for illustrating an integrated approach to understanding the spectrum of narcissism in showing where the levels are both symbiotic and interdependent, it does not in any way score the individual's level of narcissistic tendencies.

For that we need a more accurate diagnostic tool that measures the symptoms of psychopathy (i.e. lack of empathy and conscience, the grandiosity and pathological lying, the degree of violations of social norms, etc.). The most useful diagnostic tool I found for understanding the different levels of narcissistic pathological behaviour is Robert Hare's Psychopathy Checklist-Revised (PCL-R). It is currently being used by many health professionals worldwide as "the gold standard" methodology for assessing an individual's psychopathic or antisocial tendencies (Hare 2003). The checklist was originally designed by Hare in the 1990s to be used within the prison system. It consisted of two parts—a semi-structured interview, and a report of the prisoner's history and criminal records—to be used by specifically trained professionals in forensic settings for assessing the degree of severity of a convicted prisoner's psychopathic traits, their propensities for the victimization of others, and their antisocial lifestyles. The results were used for predicting the individual's future

PCL-R is a useful tool for working with survivors of narcissistic abuse.

violent behaviour, and for deciding on the type of prison sentence handed down, and in some cases, for recommending the death penalty.

Of course, diagnosing someone as a psychopath is going to have very serious implications for that person; therefore, in the interest of justice, the diagnosis, should only be assigned to someone highly trained in psychopathy and administered under stringent conditions.

I will later introduce some of the twenty criteria covered in Hare's PCL-R that is associated with assessing the depth of the perpetrator's behaviours, i.e. the severity of their glib and superficial charm, grandiosity, boredom, pathological lying, cunning and manipulation, lack of remorse or guilt, shallow emotions, callousness and lack of empathy, parasitic lifestyle, poor behavioural controls, sexual promiscuity, early behaviour problems, lack of realistic long-term goals, impulsivity, irresponsibility, failure to accept responsibility, many short-term marital relationships, juvenile delinquency, revocation of conditional release, and criminal versatility. These twenty items cover the perpetrator's interpersonal relationships, and their emotional and social involvement, and responses to situations and other people. Evidence of the individual's social deviance and their lifestyle can be scored against the twenty items with either a 0 (never), 1 (sometimes) or 2 (always), depending on how much the dysfunctional behaviour applies to the perpetrator.

> A therapist who is not informed in the full spectrum of narcissistic abuse (The Dark Triad) will probably not be able to take the victim to complete their process.

Although I am deviating somewhat from Hare's original use of his checklist, I have found the PCL-R a useful tool for working with survivors of narcissistic abuse. Even a basic understanding of this twenty-item symptom rating scale will allow psychotherapists to understand and evaluate the degree of narcissistic abuse their clients were subjected to. Using the checklist as a rough guide, a therapist could assume that a person with a healthy level of narcissism would normally score around 5, (less than 4 would represent someone scoring too low in narcissism and needing some help with self-esteem issues); 10–19 qualifies a person in the NPD range, 20–29 qualifies

MN (the sub-clinical psychopath would score from 26–29), and 30–40 is considered full-blown psychopathy. For example, the likes of Ted Bundy (who murdered thirty victims) would receive a maximum score of 40, making him a prototypical psychopath.

> Profiling the offender will give the psychotherapist and client a better understanding of the level of abuse suffered, and validating that suffering.

The reason for explaining the indicators of each of the Three Faces of Evil is not so much that therapists, or victims, can make a formal diagnosis of the perpetrator. On the contrary, it is important to leave that job to a trained professional. It is more for gaining essential insights into the level of abuse (mental, physical and psychological) experienced by the survivor, and for reframing the details of abuse so that healing can begin (Mallon).

When working with victims of narcissistic abuse, I would go as far as to say that a therapist who is not informed in the full spectrum of narcissistic abuse (The Dark Triad) will probably not be able to take the victim to complete their process. It is my belief that in order for true healing to happen, victims need a full understanding of what really happened to them. Often the client has no idea that they were in a relationship with someone with a personality disorder, and sometimes that information is like handing them the missing piece of the jigsaw puzzle that explains the madness.

A psychotherapist needs to be familiar with the Hare's Psychopathy Checklist, and use the information for educating the client. In some instances the therapist may find it a useful exercise to download Hare's Psychopathy Test and go through the twenty questions with the victim, allowing them to score their perpetrator's behaviour accordingly. Profiling the offender will give the psychotherapist and client a better understanding of the level of abuse suffered, and validating that suffering.

THE BUILDING BLOCKS OF THE PSYCHOPATHIC CHARACTER
The Emotional And Interpersonal Aspects

"In the self, good and evil are indeed closer than identical twins!"
—C.G. Jung

When it comes to understanding psychopathy, I think it is important for any therapist to understand the key symptoms found in Hare's Psychopathy Checklist (PCL-R). As mentioned earlier, Hare lists twenty items to describe his model of psychopathy; however, this chapter looks at some of the emotional and interpersonal aspects (i.e. glibness, grandiosity, lack of remorse or guilt, lack of empathy, and shallow emotions). Chapter 10 will explore some of the social deviance aspects of psychopathy.

GLIBNESS AND SUPERFICIAL CHARM

> The psychopath's superficial charm is used to acquire a victim's trust in order to con them.

When we speak of psychopaths as being glib or superficial, we are referring to the insincere and superficial charm they use to acquire a victim's trust in order to con them. Their charm makes them appear to be great listeners. They do this in order to simulate empathy while zeroing in on their targets' dreams and vulnerabilities in order to be able to manipulate them later. They are masters of seduction, both figuratively and literally, and that makes them seem more charming and more interesting than most normal people (Stout). These traits render them to appear smooth, engaging, talkative, loquacious, charming and slick to the onlooker (Hare).

Psychopaths use their glib and superficial charm with the intention of being evasive, deflect emotion, or conceal their lack of emotional depth from others. This psychopathic charm is not in the least shy or self-conscious, which results in the psychopath being unafraid to say anything if it helps their cause. They are articulate conversationalists with the "gift of the gab", and therefore capable of spinning outrageously witty, convincing stories. They are very amusing, entertaining and believable, not to mention very likable. They go on the "charm offensive" by emphasizing their charisma or trustworthiness, and turn on their superficial smile for totally disarming and seducing victims. They use their charm for getting information. Information is power to the psychopath, so the more they know about you, the more potential they have for gaining power over you.

Psychopaths have an extremely low self-consciousness, and it is this "lacking" that sets them free from the normal restraints of social and emotional impediments experienced by the general population. This means that they are more likely to present themselves well; they come across readily comfortable and relaxed when talking with other people, giving them a natural flair for putting others at ease. They typically like to present themselves as experts on many subjects in order to appear very interesting and knowledgeable.

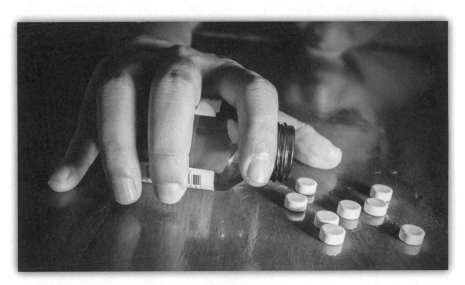

However, they are generally not able to take any subject very far, but it does not seem to matter to them if they are found out as a fraud. They deliver compliments and flattery with confidence, which manages to seduce and win most people over. Even though their tall stories should be unbelievable, somehow they have a knack of pulling the wool over the eyes of intelligent people who seem to fall for their stories. Another striking feature of psychopaths is that they have low-level feelings of vulnerability, which leads to them becoming somewhat fearless.

It is this fearlessness that makes them prone to engage in high-risk activities that area part of Hare's checklist, such as conning, crime, drugs, robbing, rape, etc. The effectiveness of these behaviours has to do with the skills of the psychopath, as well as the ability of the person perceiving the behaviour to recognise deception. But the vast majority of victims fall for the con.

GRANDIOSE SENSE OF SELF-WORTH

Psychopaths have grossly inflated views of their abilities and self-worth, and this is demonstrated in the way they are self-assured, opinionated, cocky and a braggart (Hare, 1999). Grandiosity is the cornerstone of pathological narcissism; it permeates into every aspect of the narcissist's personality. As a result, they exaggerate their talents, capacities and their achievements in an unrealistic way. Their grandiosity also leads to an unrealistic sense of superiority and entitlement—a perception that leads to them viewing others with disdain or as inferior. Because they see themselves as "unique" and "special" they feel that they can only be understood by other "special" people. They have delusional, magical fantasies and often suffer from a God complex, an unshakable belief in their personal abilities. They then believe that they are deserving of being the smartest, best looking, best dressed, and own the best car and the grandest house. They

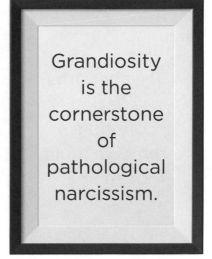

Grandiosity is the cornerstone of pathological narcissism.

constantly downgrade others in order to boost their own egos, and they hide behind a false self in order to keep the illusion going. All this leads to the psychopath behaving self-centeredly and/or self-referentially at great expense to everyone around them.

LACK OF REMORSE OR GUILT

Psychopaths lack conscience, remorse, guilt or shame. They lack feelings or concern for the loss, pain and suffering of their victims. They also have a tendency to be unconcerned, dispassionate, cold-hearted and not empathetic (Hare, 1999). This lack of conscience gives psychopaths the moral freedom to do practically whatever they like to anyone and not feel pained by what they have done. They do the most outrageous things, and then act as if nothing out of the ordinary has happened. They have no respect for the rights of others; they are only concerned with getting what they want, with no account of the cost to

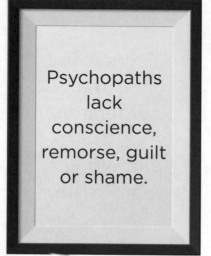

Psychopaths lack conscience, remorse, guilt or shame.

others. They do not feel the fear or anxiety that conscience can bring to most people; it is all just a game to them, but a game in which they have to be the winner. They think only of self-interests while disregarding the interests of others. In effect, others are merely instruments to be used and capitalized on for gaining personal supply. They get away with these actions because they have learned how to mimic the feelings of others, so they can act guilty, ashamed or remorseful when necessary, but in reality they never have empathy or conscience to deal with, so they are fully free to abuse by all manners of gaslighting behaviours.

LACK OF EMPATHY

Psychopaths show a lack of feelings towards people in general; they are cold, contemptuous, inconsiderate and tactless (Hare, 1999). This lack of empathy is the base of many of their characteristics—pathological lying, shallow emotions, chilling violence, shamelessness, egocentricity, lack of remorse, deceitfulness, manipulation, etc. With their empathy effectively switched "off", they callously think only about themselves.

It appears that having no empathy arises from abnormalities in the empathy circuit of the brain, leaving psychopaths underdeveloped in empathic responses. Therefore, they can be single-minded and callous, and indifferent to the rights and sufferings of others. They are as emotionally famished as androids. Without the ability to experience real emotional attachments, they have no 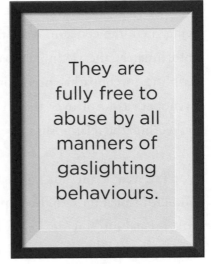 sense of moral duty to anyone beyond their own self-interests. They treat the vulnerable with disdain because psychopaths see vulnerability as weakness. To them, whoever is weak deserves to be exploited. Unbelievably, they can justify their actions, and even rationalize that they, in some way, are in fact the victim. This lack of empathy allows them to dehumanize people into mere objects to be manipulated.

Psychopathy begins early in life (in what is labelled "childhood conduct disorders"). These individuals may have tortured animals, abused family members or committed cold-blooded acts against others while growing up. It seems that this lack of empathy leaves them unable to figuratively step into the shoes of another person in order to understand and identify with their situations and feelings. It is as if psychopaths simply lack the ability to construct mental and emotional facsimiles of another person. Because of a lack of empathy, psychopaths are very drawn to highly empathic people as a source of supply.

They are fully free to abuse by all manners of gaslighting behaviours.

Empaths are able to put themselves in a narcissist's shoes, giving them the concern, warmth, comfort and attention they crave. Unfortunately, the victim's empathy also sets them up in a way that feeds the psychopathic need for power and dominance, giving the psychopath control over their victim's emotions and keeping them hooked into the relationship.

However, I am not convinced that the psychopath's empathy quotient is stuck on zero. In all probability, psychopaths know how to turn "on and off" their empathy switches, and even conflate empathy for grasping another's emotional state. This makes them more efficient when it comes to knowing which buttons to push for baiting and hooking purposes. They also seem to know how to use empathy as a solvent for resolving interpersonal problems and getting into the minds of others. In fact, their understanding of empathy allows them to use it to their own full advantage for becoming highly skilled and effective in their range and scope of abuse.

But empathy is a complex emotion, so it must be understood at the outset that people can do the most horrible things, identify closely with their victims, and learn to live with the angst that accumulates (Turvey, 2012). There are many incidents of psychopaths having shown empathy towards their victims at the scene of a crime. For example, a rapist laying down a coat for their victim, or the abductor deciding not to harm a victim when they have cried, and even returning them back to where the abduction took place. Sometimes the psychopath will agree to accommodate the victim's request, such as using a condom during a rape, untying their hands or apologizing after the offense. What the psychopath really lacks is generally a sense of compassion.

Michael Stone, a forensic psychiatrist, states that psychopaths use empathy to their advantage. Even serial killers know that when a child cries they are in distress probably because they've been separated from their mother. Where the compassionate person feels sad for the child and takes measures to reunite the two, the psychopath uses the opportunity to take the child by the hand and pretends to get them back to their mother, but instead kidnaps them (as was the case of two-year-old Jamie Bulger, who was murdered by two ten-year-old boys, Venables and Thompson).

SHALLOW EMOTIONS

Shallow emotions concern the lack of depth, quality and stability of an individual's emotional life. Despite seeming friendly, psychopaths suffer from emotional poverty (Hare, 1999); therefore, they are unable to experience emotion like the normal population. Their proto-emotions are more primitive responses to their immediate needs. For example, they do not feel fear, therefore, they do not respond with the normal responses to a threatening stimulus (i.e., trembling, sweating, heart-racing, etc.). Brain scans show that they do not respond to emotionally charged words in the normal way.

There is no sign of activity in their limbic system; their response is due to a cognitive reaction rather than an emotional reaction. They only know emotion through words, and not through experience. As a consequence, their feelings come across as shallow and confused. For example, they do not understand real love; they confuse it with sexual arousal, making their sexual relationships superficial and impersonal.

Because they are unable to form deep, emotional bonds, they cannot feel love, nor reciprocate the love they receive from others. Because they fail in the usual physiological responses to fear, this may explain their lack of understanding when they see fear in their victims' faces. Their lack of fear makes them very dangerous and feckless risk-takers, and they will carry out violent acts in a cold and dispassionate way.

The thought of pain or punishment does not deter them in any way. They show absolute indifference to hardships they bring on others, whether financial, social, emotional, physical, or other, even those they profess to love. Sometimes psychopaths will readily express feelings, emotions, and affect, but the feelings and emotions are rather limited in strength and depth of feeling, or, as psychologists J. Johns and H.C. Quay said, "They [psychopaths] know the words but not the music".

Scan this QR code to
visit www.tinyurl.com/articlecollection
and get your FREE Complete Article Collection on
Narcissistic Behaviour.

CHAPTER 10

THE BUILDING BLOCKS OF THE PSYCHOPATHIC CHARACTER
The Social Deviance Aspects

"Opening up to the idea of evil helps therapists see
and address things they may otherwise miss."
—Rollow May & Carl Rogers

I
n this chapter, we shall continue to look at Hare's Psychopathy
Checklist (PCL-R) for understanding the social deviance aspects
of the psychopathic behaviours that have a destructive impact
on victims (i.e. the impulsivity, poor behavioural control, need for
excitement, early behavioural problems, adult antisocial behaviour,
pathological lying, deceit and manipulation).

IMPULSIVITY

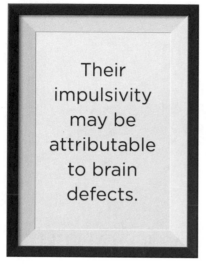

Their impulsivity may be attributable to brain defects.

Impulsivity is the occurrence of behaviours that are unpremeditated and lack reflection or planning. Being impulsive means having the inability to resist temptation, frustrations, and urges; having a lack of deliberation without considering the consequences; and engaging in behaviour that is foolhardy, rash, unpredictable, erratic and reckless (Hare). Psychopaths live in the moment, and as a result, they execute their deeds without much planning or forethought. They don't seem to fully understand the consequences of their actions, and they are generally unprepared to meet the challenges they face. Their impulsivity may be attributable to brain defects, or their need to avoid painful emotions by distracting themselves.

POOR BEHAVIOURAL CONTROLS

The characteristics of poor behavioural controls, according to Hare, refer to violent, damaging or reactionary behaviour that is not controlled, such as expressions of irritability, annoyance, impatience, threats, aggression and verbal abuse, inadequate control of anger and temper, and acting hastily, even when the consequences may be harmful to them personally. Psychopaths have wicked, explosive tempers, and verbal and aggressive outbursts are common. Often their attacks are sudden and unprovoked; one moment they are laughing, the next moment they are throwing you to the ground (physically or metaphorically speaking).

It may have been something you said or something they imagined you said. It does not take much provocation to send them into attack mode. With their inhibitory controls weak, psychopaths are short-tempered and hot headed, and once they are in a rage, it is as if they fail to consider any consequences. Their modus operandi is to act first and think later. But their outbursts are generally short lived,

Their modus operandi is to act first and think later.

and they quickly resume back to acting as if nothing unusual had happened, leaving their victim in tatters, confused and very afraid. Of course, they never take responsibility for their actions, and because it is always the other person's fault, there is no need for them to feel any sense of shame, guilt or remorse.

NEED FOR EXCITEMENT or PRONENESS TO BOREDOM

They engage in "magical thinking".

Psychopaths have an excessive need for novelty, according to Hare, they need thrilling and exciting stimulation, and they take chances and do things that are risky. Because of their proneness to boredom, they tend to become disinterested, distracted or disconnected. They tend to go in search of excitement, often in the form of new narcissistic supply. They engage in "magical thinking" because they believe that they are authoritative and therefore they will always win. This makes them fearless and relentless in pursuit of revenge—a revenge that, in their heads, will be triumphant (the God complex). All these aspects together make the psychopath highly dangerous when their sources of supply are threatened.

EARLY BEHAVIOUR PROBLEMS

A variety of problem behaviours can be seen prior to age thirteen, including lying, stealing, cheating, vandalism, bullying, sexual activity, glue-sniffing, consuming alcohol and running away (Hare). Juvenile psychopathy is increasing at an alarming rate. Evidence shows that juveniles do present with similar correlates seen in adult psychopaths. These "fledgling psychopaths" all have character disturbances.

They engage in persistent antisocial behaviour, exhibit insensitivity to punishment cues, show poor behavioural control, and have hyperactivity-impulsivity attention difficulties (Andershed), and they would be expected to get increasingly more dangerous with age.

Their childhood behaviours, such as aggression, theft, truancy, lying, poor educational achievements, drug problems, etc., all serve as good indicators of things to come at a later stage of development. Such incidents as those described have made it increasingly clear that psychopathy is not exclusively an adult manifestation. These adolescents might not become killers, but they will learn how to manipulate, deceive and exploit others for their own gain. There is a set of three behavioural characteristics used by forensic practitioners in assessing psychopathy risk, known as the "MacDonald Triad". These include childhood cruelty to animals, obsession with fire setting and persistent bedwetting past the age of twelve. These childhood behaviours have been linked to later adult violent offending (i.e. homicidal behaviour and sexually predatory behaviour), and therefore strong predictors of a childhood psychopathy.

ADULT ANTISOCIAL BEHAVIOUR

Psychopaths demonstrate their persistent violations of social norms and expectations through their prominent lack of conscience or morality that is acted out in their antisocial behaviour. They have little or no regard for societal rules, seeing them as inconvenient and unreasonable impediments to their expression of freedom. They act on impulse, not stopping to reflect on their actions, and many of their antisocial acts lead to criminal charges and convictions. Psychopaths are criminally versatile, committing diverse types of offenses.

> Psychopaths take delight in deceiving others. This is often referred to as "duping delight".

They take great pride at getting away with crimes or wrongdoings (Hare). Often sexually promiscuous, they engage in a variety of brief, superficial relations, numerous affairs, and an indiscriminate selection of sexual partners; the maintenance of numerous, multiple relationships at the same time; a history of attempts to sexually coerce others into sexual activity (rape) or taking great pride at discussing sexual exploits and conquests (Hare). Because the psychopath sees their narcissistic supply as extensions of their own selves, they see nothing wrong in sexually abusing their own children or other people's children.

PATHOLOGICAL LYING

The psychopaths' lying can be moderate or high. In moderate form, they will be shrewd, crafty, cunning, sly and clever; in extreme form, they will be deceptive, deceitful, underhanded, unscrupulous, manipulative and dishonest (Hare). Psychopaths lie by both commission and omission. They either say things that are untruthful or leave things out, distorting the truth. Because they have no conscience and can lie with great confidence in order to con, manipulate and control people, psychopaths take delight in deceiving others. This is often referred to as "duping delight" (Paul Ekman), which serves to excite them and reinforce their narcissistic delusions.

Psychopaths are obsessed with one-upmanship, and have an overpowering need to be better than everyone else. They always need to be "right", and will always argue the point rather than admit that they are wrong. Being wrong only serves to threaten their fantasies of themselves.

They have little or no value for the truth, but to challenge them on a lie only sends them into defensive behaviour where you are likely to meet their extreme displays of rage. They like to convince people to confide in them, but since they do not value loyalty, they will also not honour the confidentiality that you may think you have with them. For them, "knowledge is power". So if what you have told them serves their purposes in gaining something for themselves, not only will they tell others, but they will embellish these stories in order to make you look worse.

They are somewhat hypochondriac, and this can come in especially useful when caught in a lie. For example, they can claim that they have been sick or have been stressed, but it's simply another excuse tool for their behaviour. They are also masses of contradictions, saying something one day and retracting it the next (because they cannot keep up with their own lies). They will act very defensively when you question them about the discrepancies. They will go to great lengths to get sympathy, lying about what others have supposedly done to them. They will oftentimes even believe the lies that are coming out of their own mouths.

DECEIT AND MANIPULATION

The characteristics of deceit and manipulation make psychopaths masters at discovering weaknesses in others. They will exploit any opportunities for their own gains (i.e., conning, cheating, defrauding, or exploiting), and carry it off in a cool, self-assured, brazen manner, with no concern or remorse for their victims. They believe that the world is made up of predators and prey, and they are out to get you before you get them.

They use deception to get close to victims, and then use their victims' emotions and beliefs against them. They will deliberately make friends with people in order to get close to their friends, and then beg, borrow or extort money from them.

They seduce victims and put them in a mesmerized state where they can have power and control over them with relative ease. Lulled into a false state of intimacy, the victim's oxytocin (the psychopath) takes over. Once hooked, the psychopath is able to put the betrayal bond in place, making it hard for victims to escape.

CONCLUSION

From each of the criteria above it is clear to see that psychopathy is more than the sum of its parts, but a synergy of different elements working together through the Dark Triad that includes all the criteria of narcissism, Machiavellianism and psychopathy. The only thing separating these three personality types is one of degree. Regardless of what criteria you look at, what remains constant is the pathological narcissist's ever-present behaviours: the cunning and manipulation, the lack of remorse or guilt, the grandiose estimation of self, the lack of empathy, the need for attention and entitlement, the pathological lying, the need for stimulation, the flaunting of rules, the self-centeredness, the shallow affect, the callousness, the need for power and control, the shame proneness and the rages.

What I have attempted to demonstrate throughout these chapters is a practical way for ordinary people to distinguish normal, healthy narcissism from pathological narcissism in order to remain safe. *The Three Faces Of Evil* offers a glimpse at the full psychology of narcissism, a multiple view that is defined through the Dark Triad of personality. These three personality types overlap somewhat, and they are all manipulative and callous with their own particular strategies and behaviours. For example, pathological narcissism allows the individual to be very charming on their initial contact with the chosen victim, allowing them to make a first great impression for establishing the "idealized stage" of the relationship. The malignant narcissist (with their Machiavellian ways) makes a cruel strategist that tears down the opponent by any means available during the "devaluing stage". Finally, we come to psychopathy, the most chilling and pathological of all the faces of evil. The psychopath, with a heart of darkness that is devoid of conscience, hovers at the edge of their humanity. With little or no regard for the life of others, the "discarding phase" will end tragically in the cold-blooded murder of either the victim's body, mind or soul.

Within the general population, approximately 1% are diagnosed as pure, full-blown psychopaths, not all of whom are locked up in jail or mental institutions. However, even more worrying is the estimated 4% of un-diagnosed sub-clinical psychopaths who wear a mask of normalcy and live amongst us daily.

Most people probably know one psychopath, but would not have a clue how to identify them; however, the clues are only invisible when you don't know what to look for. When most people think of psychopaths (male and female) they think of the characters they see in the movies like *Silence of the Lambs, Peeping Tom, The Night of the Hunter, Cape Fear, Misery, Fatal Attraction, Basic Instinct* and the Joker character from Batman.

Most people equate female psychopaths such as Rosemary West, Andrea Yates, and Diana Downs, and male psychopaths such as Fred West, John Wayne Gacy, Jr. Theodore Bundy, Jack the Ripper, etc., as stereotypical psychopaths. But this is far from the truth. Yes, all of these people mentioned above are psychopaths who have murdered, but it must be remembered that each lived and fit into their communities as ordinary people long before being caught. They were accepted as mothers and fathers, brothers and sisters, husbands and wives, sons and daughters, friends and neighbours, and bosses and workmates by

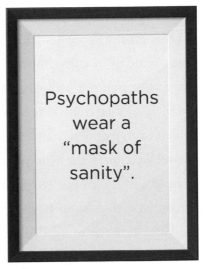

Psychopaths wear a "mask of sanity".

those people who knew them. It is important to know that not all psychopaths morph into criminals or serial killers. According to forensic psychiatrist Michael Welner, psychopaths wear a "mask of sanity" which they present to the outside world, and it is this mask that allows most psychopaths to lead ordinary lives, just like the rest of us.

The mask of respectability makes it hard to spot them, especially if they hold responsible positions such as CEOs, teachers, physicians, surgeons, lawyers, counsellors, priests, business executives, engineers, etc. Psychopathy has never been as evident as it is today. It can be seen in the flagitious behaviour within organizations (banks, churches, corporations, hospitals, colleges, governments, therapy-training courses, cults, care homes, etc.). The most disturbing thing to grasp is that the perpetrators of these crimes are not mad; their crimes are cold, calculated, rational manipulation that is driven by greed and a lack of conscience and remorse.

If you were to believe in a movie's portrayal of a psychopath, you may be misled to believe that psychopaths are all serial killers. The truth is that most psychopaths ply their trade through other means, which threaten the ordinary person's psychological functioning. The majority of shattered victims that I see in my therapy room have been subjected to pathological narcissistic abuse, either in their homes, their friendships, or in the workplace. With the exception of a scarce few, none could figure out what had happened to them. So in order to protect ourselves from having similar experiences with a psychopath that may be close to us, it is crucial that we learn how to identify the behaviours that betray them.

I am often asked, "How come you do not hate your brother?" All I can answer is that when I was thirteen I saw the film *Pollyanna* with Hailey Mills, I could identify with her totally, and her "Glad Game". At one point in the film, Pollyanna says, "There is something about everything that you can be glad about if you keep hunting long enough to find it." Well, I am "glad" for my life, for the family I had, and the love I had for Gerard in between all the madness. God knows that I hunted long enough for the knowledge and wisdom to make the most of my learnings, which have giving meaning to my life.

Gerard was a big factor in my realising my life's mission, so I am grateful to him for that. Because of him, I can truly say that when a client comes into my therapy room with the cluster of symptoms that I mentioned earlier, and tells me a story such as I have described of my own life, I would know that they were indeed likely to be suffering from narcissistic victim syndrome (NVS).

I made a vow that I would make it my mission to do my best to relieve the pain and suffering of narcissistic abuse by providing information and education for those professionals who deal with the fallout of this form of abuse. Unfortunately, as yet, there is not a comprehensive psychology of the whole spectrum of narcissism for therapists to work from. Because therapists are trained to be compassionate, it was necessary to place the focus of this psychology on the concept of evil for giving the therapist another lens to see through, providing a better therapeutic vision for working with victims who often speak of having been impacted by evil.

This book focuses on the pathological behaviours of the narcissist, but this is only one side of the argument. My next book will be dedicated to the victims and how they are affected by narcissistic abuse. It is important for therapists working with victims to understand that the sequelae of narcissistic abuse may include any of the following symptoms: low self-esteem, self-mutilation (self-harming), repressed memories, panic attacks, suicidal thought, chronic pain, CPTSD, depression and somatisation disorders.

Of course, any of these symptoms mentioned may be found in any client; however when they present themselves in a cluster, the psychotherapist will start to identify narcissistic victim syndrome emerging. These victims are also likely to demonstrate feelings of shame, humiliation, over-responsibility, self-blame, guilt, powerlessness and inadequacy. Many will have been re-victimized by more than one narcissist during their life. But there are more complicated symptoms that will be revealed and explained in my next book.

SUGGESTED READING

Almaas, A. H.1996 . *The Point of Existence* Berkeley, CA: Diamond Books.

American Psychiatric Association (1994) *Diagnostic and Statistical Manual of Mental Disorders, fourth edition.* Washington, DC. American Psychiatric Association.

Blair, J. Mitchell, D. & Blair, K. (2005). *The Psychopath: Emotion and the Brain.* Blackwell Publishing.

Bowlby, J. (1979). The *Making and Breaking of Affectional Bonds.* Tavistock Publications.

Carnes, P.J. (1997). *The Betrayal Bond: Breaking Free of Exploitive Relationships.*

Deerfield Beach: Health Communications, Inc.

Cleckley, Harvey M. (1988). *The Mask of Sanity: An Attempt to Clarify Some Issues About the So Called Psychopathic Personality.* Library of Congress Cataloguing in Publication Data.

Dutton, D. G. & Painter, S. (1993). *Emotional Attachments in Abusive Relationships: A Test of the Traumatic Bonding Theory.* Violence and Victims, Vol. 8, No. 2,1993 © 1993 Springer Publishing Companypp.105-120.

Fromm, E. (1964). *The Heart of Man.* Harper and Row.

Fallon, J. (2013). *The Psychopath Inside: A Neuroscientist's Personal Journey into the Dark Side of the Brain.* Current (Penguin Group), pp. 60; 72; 76; 79.

Farrington, D.P. (1989). *Early predictors of adolescent aggression and adult violence.* Violence and Victims 4:79-100.

Goldner. & Moore. (2010). *MALIGNANT NARCISSISM: From Fairy Tales to Harsh Reality.* Psychiatria Danubina, 2010; Vol. 22, No. 3, pp. 392–405.

Graham, D. L., Rawlings, E., & Rimini, N. (1988). *Survivors of Terror.* In Y. Yllo and M. Bograd's (eds.) *Feminists perspectives on wife abuse.* Newbury Park, CA: Sage Publications, Inc.

Grof, S. (1985). *Beyond the Brain: Birth, Death, and Transendence in Psychotherapy.* University of New York. pp. 79; 111; 157; 215.

Grof, S. (1988). *The Adventure of Self-Discovery: Dimensions of Consciousness and New Perspectives in Psychotherapy and Inner Exploration.* (Suny Series in Transpersonal and Humanistic Psychology). State University of New York Press.

Gottfredson, Michael, R., &Hirschi, Travis. (1990). *A General Theory of Crime.*, Stanford, CA: Stanford University Press, 1990, xvi pp. 297.

Hare, R. (1999). *Without Conscience: The Disturbing World of the Psychopaths Among Us.* The Gilford Press. New York. Audio book: 6hrs:53mins.

Hare, R.D. (2003). *The Hare Psychopathy Checklist-Revised (2nd ed.).* Toronto: Multi-Health Systems.

Hare, R. D., & Neumann, C. S. (2006). *The PCL-R Assessment of Psychopathy: Development, Structural properties, and New Directions.* In C. Patrick (Ed.), Handbook of psychopathy. New York: Guilford Press. pp. 58–90.

Kernberg, Otto F. (1980). *Internal World and External Reality.* Aronson, J. H. p.108.

Locke, John. (1996). *An Essay Concerning Human Understanding.* Kenneth P. Winkler (Ed.), Hackett Publishing Company, Indianapolis, IN, pp. 33-36.

Lowen, A. (1997). *Narcissism: Denial of the True Self.* Touchstone.

March, W. (1954). *The Bad Seed.* Rinehart & Company.

Millon, T. Grossman, Millon. Meagher. & Ramnath. (2004). *Personality Disorders in Modern Life, Second Edition.* John Miley & Son.

Moffitt, T.E. (1993). *Adolescents-Limited and Life-Course-Persistent Antisocial Behaviour: A Developmental Taxonomy.* Psychological Review, pp.100; 674-701.

Moffitt, T.E., Lynam, D. and Silva, P.A. (1994). *Neuropsychological Tests Predict Persistent Make Delinquency.* Criminology 32 (2): pp. 101-124.

Morf and Rhodewalt. (2001). *Unraveling the Paradoxes of Narcissism: A Dynamic Self-Regulatory Processing Model.* Psychological Inquiry 2001, Vol. 12, No. 4, pp. 177–196.

Morley, K., & Hall, W. (2003). *Is There A Genetic Susceptibility To Engage In Criminal Acts?* Australian Institute of Criminology: Trends and Issues in Crime and Criminal Justice, pp. 263, 1-6.

Patrick, C. J.(1994*). Emotion and Psychopathy: Startling New Insights.* Psychophysiology*, pp. 31, 319-330.*

Patrick, C. (Editor), (2006). *Handbook of Psychopathy*, The Gilford Press.

Raine, A. Brennan, P.A., Farrington. D.P. & Mednick, S.D. (1997). *Bopsocial Bases of Violence,* New York: Plenum Press.

Ronningstam, E. (2005). *Identifying and Understanding the Narcissistic Personality.* Oxford University Press.

Schouten, R. (2012). *Almost a Psychopath: Do I (or Does Someone I Know) Have a Problem with Manipulation and Lack of Empathy?* Harvard University.

Salekin, R. T. (2002). *Psychopathy and Therapeutic Pessimism: Clinical Lore or Clinical Reality?* Clinical Psychology Review, pp. 22,79–112.

Simon, G.K. (2010). *Understanding and Dealing with Manipulative People.* Parkhurst Brothers, Ink.

Stout, M. (2005). *The Sociopath Next Door.* Broadway Books.

Turvey, B. (2012). *Criminal Profiling: An Introduction to Behavioral Evidence Analysis.* Elsevier Pub. Ltd.

Twenge, J. M. & Campbell, W. K. (2009). *The Narcissism Epidemic Living in the Age of Entitlement.* Free Press.

Vaknin, S. (2003). *Malignant Self Love: Narcissism Revisited.* Barnes & Noble.

Wong, S., & Hare, R. D. (2005). *Guidelines for a Psychopathy Treatment Program.* Toronto, ON: Multi Health Systems. pp. 371.

116

RESOURCES: WEBSITES

www.Narcissisticbehavior.net

www.Outofthefog.net

www.Saferelationshipsmagazine.com

www.Narcissismfree.com

www.Willieverbegoodenough.com/narcissistic-mother

www.Narcissismfree.com

www.Psychopathyawareness.wordpress.com

www.Lovefraud.com

www.Drjoecarver.com

www.Psychopathfree.com

www.Narcissisticmother.com

www.Selfcarehaven.wordpress.com

ABOUT THE AUTHOR

Christine Louis de Canonville's educational background includes a B.A. Hons in Psychology and Theology. She is an accredited Humanistic and Integrative Psychotherapist; Master Clinical Hypnotherapist; Master NLP Practitioner; Life, Executive & Business Coach; Transpersonal Psychotherapist, Clinical Supervisor, Trainer and Theologian. She also holds a Diploma in Forensic Psychology; Diploma in Criminology; and is a registered Teacher with the Irish Teaching Council of Ireland. She studied for a Masters Degree in Medical Anthropology, doing her fieldwork with indigenous shamans.

She worked with victims in St. Brendan's Psychiatric Hospital in the PTSD Unit. She has had her own private practice for 20 years, where she has integrated both Eastern and Western therapies for providing a holistic way of working with victims of narcissistic abuse, mentally, emotionally and spiritually. Christine resides in Dublin, Ireland.

To contact Christine, please email: christine@narcissisticbehavior.net.

For more information please visit Christine's website: www.narcissisticbehavior.net

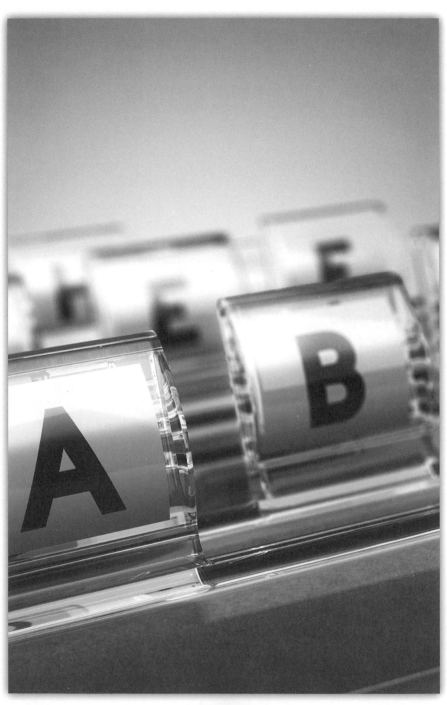

INDEX

Abandonment, 7, 19, 37, 41, 47, 50

Boundaries, 26, 33, 43

Conscience, 28, 32, 35, 47, 49, 46, 59, 66, 68, 78, 89, 90, 106

Control, 6, 7, 8, 14, 15, 17, 26, 37, 46, 49, 56, 57, 59, 60, 61, 62, 68, 74, 79, 97, 98, 99, 101, 103, 104

Dark Triad, 4, 5, 65, 82, 105

Devalue, 26, 34, 46, 54

Discarding, 45, 63, 106

Empathy, 1, 26, 29, 39, 41, 43, 47, 54, 55, 56, 62, 68, 74, 78, 79, 85, 86, 90, 91, 92, 93

Entitlement, 43, 47, 51, 57, 88, 105

Envious, 25, 26, 41, 43, 55

Gaslighting, 13, 44, 90

Grandiosity, 33, 39, 78, 79, 85, 88

Hare's Psychopathy Checklist-Revised (PCL-R), 32, 77

Machiavellianism, 33, 55, 105, 106

Manipulation, 36, 45, 71, 79, 90, 97, 104, 105, 107

Narcissism, 3, 4, 5, 21, 22, 23, 24, 25, 27, 28, 29, 31, 34, 36, 39, 41, 49, 51, 54 55, 56, 65, 70, 73, 77, 78,80, 88, 105, 109

Narcissistic supply, 18, 31, 32, 33, 47, 58, 61, 62, 100, 102

Power, 6, 8, 14, 15, 17, 26, 40, 43, 46, 54, 55, 59, 60, 62, 63, 87, 92, 103, 104, 105

Psychopath, 3, 5, 6, 9, 51, 58, 59, 63, 65, 66, 67, 68, 69, 70, 71,72 73, 74, 75, 76, 77, 78, 79, 81, 86, 87, 88, 89, 90, 91, 92, 93, 95, 98, 99, 100, 101, 102, 103, 104, 105, 106, 107, 108

Psychopathy, 3, 4, 5, 12, 32, 51,65, 66, 67, 69, 70, 71, 73, 74, 75, 77, 78, 79, 81, 83, 85, 91, 97, 100, 101, 105, 106, 107

Rage, 7, 14 , 17, 19, 33, 35, 37, 45, 47, 58, 63, 99, 103

Rejection, 7, 37, 41, 47, 49, 57

Sadistic, 2, 7, 8, 35, 51

Shame, 8, 14, 26, 33, 34, 35, 44, 45, 55, 57, 89, 99, 105, 109

Superior, 26, 33, 40,42, 43, 45, 56, 57, 63

Victims, 2, 12, 31, 44, 59, 74, 82, 87, 97, 108, 109

Last
Chance
Animals
Ireland

Volunteers devoted to saving the lives of those in need - Man's Best Friend!

We are a group of animal lovers based in Dublin, Ireland. We re-home animals all over Ireland and achieve this through a dedicated network of fosterers, volunteers and supporters who perform home checks, transport animals and donate funds towards vet bills.

Our aim is to save as many dogs and cats as possible from a life of neglect and misery.

We are a non-profit organisation. All contributions go towards helping animals in our care.

If you have a query or want to help please get in touch via
email: **lastchanceanimals@gmail.com**

Donate Today
www.lastchanceanimalsireland.com

Follow us on
Facebook
www.facebook.com/LastChanceAnimals

PLEASE
ADOPT
ME!

PLease
Rescue
Me!

Some of the proceeds from the sale of this book will be donated to **Last Chance Animals Ireland**. "Thank you for helping, Christine."

OTHER BOOKS FROM BLACK CARD BOOKS

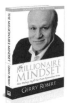

The Millionaire Mindset
*How Ordinary People Can
Create Extraordinary Income*
Gerry Robert

ISBN: 978-1-927411-00-1

CHAOS
*How Business Leaders Can
Master the Power of Focus*
James M. Burgess

ISBN: 978-3-161484-10-0

Messy Manager
*Double Your Sales
and Triple Your Profits*
Jean-Guy Francoeur

ISBN: 978-0-9786-663-0-9

The ACE Model
*Winning Formula for
Audit Committees*
Sindi Zilwa

ISBN: 978-1-927892-24-4

Mealtimes Without Mayhem
*The Easy to Follow, How to
Guidebook to Get Your Family
to Eat Together*
Jo Turner

ISBN: 978-1-927411-04-9

Creative Culture
*The Heart and Soul
of South Africa*
Bathandwa Mcuba

ISBN: 978-1-927411-65-0

Is This It?
*How Successful People Get
More Life Out of Life*
Adam Fitzpatrick

ISBN: 978-1-927411-02-5

TIME IS UP!
*How to Stop Procrastination
and Start Achieving Your
Goals*
Berns David Lucanas

ISBN: 978-1-927892-47-3

OTHER BOOKS FROM BLACK CARD BOOKS

MAXIMized Health
The New, Intelligent System for Optimum Digestion and Hormones
Dr. Andrea Maxim, ND

ISBN: 978-1-927892-06-0

STOP EXERCISING! The Way You Are Doing It Now
7 Dangerous Facts That Will Cause You to Stay Fat or Hurt Yourself
Igor Klibanov

ISBN: 978-1-927411-52-0

Liftoff
The Secret Keys to Launching Your Goals
Stanley Beckett

ISBN: 970-1-927802-18-3

APPSOLUTELY
How Anyone Can Absolutely Create a Money Making App in 10 Days or Less
Lim Tianyi

ISBN: 978-1-927892-41-1

The Power Of Pets
7 Effective Tools For Healing From Pet Loss
Marybeth Haines

ISBN: 978-1-927411-07-0

Work Hard, Die Poor? Or Work Smart, Retire Young and Rich?
Get Real & Get Rich
Alexander Woo

ISBN: 978-1-927892-46-6

Getting to SOLD
Insider Secrets to Selling Your House Fast and For Top Dollar
Analena Rebelo

ISBN: 978-1-927892-11-4

SUITE LIVING
Hotel Quality Designs for Your Home
Sheryll M. Pura

ISBN: 978-1-927892-04-6

OTHER BOOKS FROM BLACK CARD BOOKS

Discover CAMBODIA
Muslim-Friendly Backpacking
The Complete Halal
Guidebook to Safe, Fun &
Independent Travel
Yvonne Kwang & Alex Nyew

ISBN: 978-1-927411-47-6

LIFE MAKEOVER
Things I Wish My Dad
Had Taught Me About Life
Tan Choon Kiang

ISBN: 978-1-927892-02-2

Build A Money Machine
Make Money Online, Escape
the 9-5, and Be Financially
Free
Peng Joon

ISBN: 978-1-927411-51-3

THE P31 WORKSHOP™
Putting Proverbs 31 to Work
to Create Abundant HEALTH,
WEALTH AND BEAUTY
Emma Soy

ISBN: 978-1-927411-34-6

RELATIONSHIP ROI
How Associations, Charities,
and Entrepreneurs Hit
Financial Targets
Nikki Pett

ISBN: 978-1-927411-12-4

THE BIG PAY OFF
Pay Off Your Mortgage Years
Earlier Without Making More
Money Or Changing Your
Lifestyle
Itay Avni

ISBN: 978-1-927411-23-0

Calmness
Find the Calm in the Storm
and Enjoy Life Now
Helga DeSousa

ISBN: 978-1-927411-53-7

**Ground Work before
Pound Work**
Creating Life Changes from
the Inside Out
Marilyn Pierce

ISBN: 978-1-927892-80-0